PREFACE

This little book aims to give a certain perspective on the subject of language rather than to assemble facts about it. It has little to say of the ultimate psychological basis of speech and gives only enough of the actual descriptive or historical facts of particular languages to illustrate principles. Its main purpose is to show what I conceive language to be, what is its variability in place and time, and what are its relations to other fundamental human interests—the problem of thought, the nature of the historical process, race, culture, art.

The perspective thus gained will be useful, I hope, both to linguistic students and to the outside public that is half inclined to dismiss linguistic notions as the private pedantries of essentially idle minds. Knowledge of the wider relations of their science is essential to professional students of language if they are to be saved from a sterile and purely technical attitude. Among contemporary writers of influence on liberal thought Croce is one of the very few who have gained an understanding of the fundamental significance of language. He has pointed out its close relation to the problem of art. I am deeply indebted to him for this insight. Quite aside from their intrinsic interest, linguistic forms and historical processes have the greatest possible diagnostic value for the understanding of some of the more difficult and elusive problems in the psychology of thought and in the strange, cumulative drift in the life of the human spirit that we call history or progress or evolution. This value depends chiefly on the unconscious and unrationalized nature of linguistic structure.

I have avoided most of the technical terms and all of the technical symbols of the linguistic academy. There is not a single diacritical mark in the book. Where possible, the discussion is based on English material. It was necessary, however, for the scheme of the book, which includes a consideration of the protean forms in which human thought has found expression, to quote some exotic instances. For these no apology seems necessary. Owing to limitations of space I have had to leave out many ideas or principles that I should have liked to touch upon. Other points have had to be barely hinted at in a sentence or flying phrase. Nevertheless, I trust that enough has here been brought together to serve as a stimulus for the more fundamental study of a neglected field.

I desire to express my cordial appreciation of the friendly advice and helpful suggestions of a number of friends who have read the work in manuscript, notably Profs. A. L. Kroeber and R. H. Lowie of the University of California, Prof. W. D. Wallis of Reed College, and Prof. J. Zeitlin of the University of Illinois.

EDWARD SAPIR.

CONTENTS

PREFACE

CHAPTER

I. INTRODUCTORY: LANGUAGE DEFINED

Language a cultural, not a biologically inherited, function. Futility of interjectional and sound-imitative theories of the origin of speech. Definition of language. The psycho-physical basis of speech. Concepts and language. Is thought possible without language? Abbreviations and transfers of the speech process. The universality of language.

II. THE ELEMENTS OF SPEECH

Sounds not properly elements of speech. Words and significant parts of words (radical elements, grammatical elements). Types of words. The word a formal, not a functional unit. The word has a real psychological existence. The sentence. The cognitive, volitional, and emotional aspects of speech. Feeling-tones of words.

III. The Sounds of Language

The vast number of possible sounds. The articulating organs and their share in the production of speech sounds: lungs, glottal cords, nose, mouth and its parts. Vowel articulations. How and where consonants are articulated. The phonetic habits of a language. The "values" of sounds. Phonetic patterns.

IV. Form in Language: Grammatical Processes

Formal processes as distinct from grammatical functions. Intercrossing of the two points of view. Six main types of grammatical process. Word sequence as a method. Compounding of radical elements. Affixing: prefixes and suffixes; infixes. Internal vocalic change; consonantal change. Reduplication. Functional variations of stress; of pitch.

V. Form in Language: Grammatical Concepts

Analysis of a typical English sentence. Types of concepts illustrated by it. Inconsistent expression of analogous concepts. How the same sentence may be expressed in other languages with striking differences in the selection and grouping of concepts. Essential and non-essential concepts. The mixing of essential relational concepts with secondary ones of more concrete order. Form for form's sake. Classification of linguistic concepts: basic or concrete, derivational, concrete relational, pure relational. Tendency for these types of concepts to flow into each other. Categories expressed in various grammatical systems. Order and stress as relating principles in the sentence. Concord. Parts of speech: no absolute classification possible; noun and verb.

VI. Types of Linguistic Structure

The possibility of classifying languages. Difficulties. Classification into form-languages and formless languages not valid. Classification according to formal processes used not practicable. Classification according to degree of synthesis. "Inflective" and "agglutinative." Fusion and symbolism as linguistic techniques. Agglutination. "Inflective" a confused term. Threefold classification suggested: what types of concepts are expressed? what is the prevailing technique? what is the degree of synthesis? Four fundamental conceptual types. Examples tabulated. Historical test of the validity of the suggested conceptual classification.

VII. Language as a Historical Product: Drift

Variability of language. Individual and dialectic variations. Time variation or "drift." How dialects arise. Linguistic stocks. Direction or "slope" of linguistic drift. Tendencies illustrated in an English sentence. Hesitations of usage as symptomatic of the direction of drift. Leveling tendencies in English. Weakening of case elements. Tendency to fixed position in the sentence. Drift toward the invariable word.

VIII. LANGUAGE AS A HISTORICAL PRODUCT: PHONETIC LAW

Parallels in drift in related languages. Phonetic law as illustrated in the history of certain English and German vowels and consonants. Regularity of phonetic law. Shifting of sounds without destruction of phonetic pattern. Difficulty of explaining the nature of phonetic drifts. Vowel mutation in English and German. Morphological influence on phonetic change. Analogical levelings to offset irregularities produced by phonetic laws. New morphological features due to phonetic change.

IX. HOW LANGUAGES INFLUENCE EACH OTHER

Linguistic influences due to cultural contact. Borrowing of words. Resistances to borrowing. Phonetic modification of borrowed words. Phonetic interinfluencings of neighboring languages. Morphological borrowings. Morphological resemblances as vestiges of genetic relationship.

X. LANGUAGE, RACE, AND CULTURE

Naïve tendency to consider linguistic, racial, and cultural groupings as congruent. Race and language need not correspond. Cultural and linguistic boundaries not identical. Coincidences between linguistic cleavages and those of language and culture due to historical, not intrinsic psychological, causes. Language does not in any deep sense "reflect" culture.

XI. LANGUAGE AND LITERATURE

Language as the material or medium of literature. Literature may move on the generalized linguistic plane or may be inseparable from specific linguistic conditions. Language as a collective art. Necessary esthetic advantages or limitations in any language. Style as conditioned by inherent features of the language. Prosody as conditioned by the phonetic dynamics of a language.

I

Introductory: Language Defined

Speech is so familiar a feature of daily life that we rarely pause to define it. It seems as natural to man as walking, and only less so than breathing. Yet it needs but a moment's reflection to convince us that this naturalness of speech is but an illusory feeling. The process of acquiring speech is, in sober fact, an utterly different sort of thing from the process of learning to walk. In the case of the latter function, culture, in other words, the traditional body of social usage, is not seriously brought into play. The child is individually equipped, by the complex set of factors that we term biological heredity, to make all the needed muscular and nervous adjustments that result in walking. Indeed, the very conformation of these muscles and of the appropriate parts of the nervous system may be said to be primarily adapted to the movements made in walking and in similar activities. In a very real sense the normal human being is predestined to walk, not because his elders will assist him to learn the art, but because his organism is prepared from birth, or even from the moment of conception, to take on all those expenditures of nervous energy and all those muscular adaptations that result in walking. To put it concisely, walking is an inherent, biological function of man.

Not so language. It is of course true that in a certain sense the individual is predestined to talk, but that is due entirely to the circumstance that he is born not merely in nature, but in the lap of a society that is certain, reasonably certain, to lead him to its traditions. Eliminate society and there is every reason to believe that he will learn to walk, if, indeed, he survives at all. But it is just as certain that he will never learn to talk, that is, to communicate ideas according to the traditional system of a particular society. Or, again, remove the new-born individual from the social environment into which he has come and transplant him to an utterly alien one. He will develop the art of walking in his new environment very much as he would have developed it in the old. But his speech will be completely at variance with the speech of his native environment. Walking, then, is a general human activity that varies only within circumscribed limits as we pass from individual to individual. Its variability is involuntary and purposeless. Speech is a human activity that varies without assignable limit as we pass from social group to social group, because it is a purely historical heritage of the group, the product of long-continued social usage. It varies as all creative effort varies—not as consciously, perhaps, but none the less as truly as do the religions, the beliefs, the customs, and the arts of different peoples. Walking is an organic, an instinctive, function (not, of course, itself an instinct); speech is a non-instinctive, acquired, "cultural" function.

There is one fact that has frequently tended to prevent the recognition of language as a merely conventional system of sound symbols, that has seduced the popular mind into attributing to it an instinctive basis that it does not really possess. This is the well-known observation that under the stress of emotion, say of a sudden twinge of pain or of unbridled joy, we do involuntarily give utterance to sounds that the hearer interprets as indicative of the emotion itself. But there is all the difference in the world between such involuntary expression of feeling and the normal type of communication of ideas that is speech. The former kind of utterance is indeed instinctive, but it is non-symbolic; in other words, the sound of pain or the sound of joy does not, as such, indicate the emotion, it does not stand aloof, as it were, and announce that such and such an emotion is being felt. What it does is to serve as a more or less automatic overflow of the emotional energy; in a sense, it is part and parcel of the emotion itself. Moreover, such instinctive cries hardly constitute communication in any strict sense. They are not addressed to any one, they are merely overheard, if heard at all, as the bark of a dog, the sound of approaching footsteps, or the rustling of the wind is heard. If they convey certain ideas to the hearer, it is only in the very general sense in which any and every sound or even any phenomenon in our environment may be said to convey an idea to the perceiving mind. If the involuntary cry of pain which is conventionally represented by "Oh!" be looked upon as a true speech symbol equivalent to some such idea as "I am in great pain," it is just as allowable to interpret the appearance of clouds as an equivalent symbol that carries the definite message "It is likely to rain." A definition of language, however, that is so extended as to cover every type of inference becomes utterly meaningless.

The mistake must not be made of identifying our conventional interjections (our oh! and ah! and sh!) with the instinctive cries themselves.

These interjections are merely conventional fixations of the natural sounds. They therefore differ widely in various languages in accordance with the specific phonetic genius of each of these. As such they may be considered an integral portion of speech, in the properly cultural sense of the term, being no more identical with the instinctive cries themselves than such words as "cuckoo" and "kill-deer" are identical with the cries of the birds they denote or than Rossini's treatment of a storm in the overture to "William Tell" is in fact a storm. In other words, the interjections and sound-imitative words of normal speech are related to their natural prototypes as is art, a purely social or cultural thing, to nature. It may be objected that, though the interjections differ somewhat as we pass from language to language, they do nevertheless offer striking family resemblances and may therefore be looked upon as having grown up out of a common instinctive base. But their case is nowise different from that, say, of the varying national modes of pictorial representation. A Japanese picture of a hill both differs from and resembles a typical modern European painting of the same kind of hill. Both are suggested by and both "imitate" the same natural feature. Neither the one nor the other is the same thing as, or, in any intelligible sense, a direct outgrowth of, this natural feature. The two modes of representation are not identical because they proceed from differing historical traditions, are executed with differing pictorial techniques. The interjections of Japanese and English are, just so, suggested by a common natural prototype, the instinctive cries, and are thus unavoidably suggestive of each other. They differ, now greatly, now but little, because they are builded out of historically diverse materials or techniques, the respective linguistic traditions, phonetic systems, speech habits of the two peoples. Yet the instinctive cries as such are practically identical for all humanity, just as the human skeleton or nervous system is to all intents and purposes a "fixed," that is, an only slightly and "accidentally" variable, feature of man's organism.

Interjections are among the least important of speech elements. Their discussion is valuable mainly because it can be shown that even they, avowedly the nearest of all language sounds to instinctive utterance, are only superficially of an instinctive nature. Were it therefore possible to demonstrate that the whole of language is traceable, in its ultimate historical and psychological foundations, to the interjections, it would still not follow that language is an instinctive activity. But, as a matter of fact, all attempts so to explain the origin of speech have been fruitless. There is no tangible evidence, historical or otherwise, tending to show that the mass of speech elements and speech processes has evolved out of the interjections. These are a very small and functionally insignificant proportion of the vocabulary of language; at no time and in no linguistic province that we have record of do we see a noticeable tendency towards their elaboration into the primary warp and woof of language. They are never more, at best, than a decorative edging to the ample, complex fabric.

What applies to the interjections applies with even greater force to the sound-imitative words. Such words as "whippoorwill," "to mew," "to caw" are in no sense natural sounds that man has instinctively or automatically reproduced. They are just as truly creations of the human mind, flights of the human fancy, as anything else in language. They do not directly grow out of nature, they are suggested by it and play with it. Hence the onomatopoetic theory of the origin of speech, the theory that would explain all speech as a gradual evolution from sounds of an imitative character, really brings us no nearer to the instinctive level than is language as we know it to-day. As to the theory itself, it is scarcely more credible than its interjectional counterpart. It is true that a number of words which we do not now feel to have a sound-imitative value can be shown to have once had a phonetic form that strongly suggests their origin as imitations of natural sounds. Such is the English word "to laugh." For all that, it is quite impossible to show, nor does it seem intrinsically reasonable to suppose, that more than a negligible proportion of the elements of speech or anything at all of its formal apparatus is derivable from an onomatopoetic source. However much we may be disposed on general principles to assign a fundamental importance in the languages of primitive peoples to the imitation of natural sounds, the actual fact of the matter is that these languages show no particular preference for imitative words. Among the most primitive peoples of aboriginal America, the Athabaskan tribes of the Mackenzie River speak languages in which such words seem to be nearly or entirely absent, while they are used freely enough in languages as sophisticated as English and German. Such an instance shows how little the essential nature of speech is concerned with the mere imitation of things.

The way is now cleared for a serviceable definition of language. Language is a purely human and non-instinctive method of communicating ideas, emotions, and desires by means of a system of voluntarily produced symbols. These symbols are, in the first instance, auditory and they are produced by the so-called "organs of speech." There is no discernible instinctive basis in human speech as such, however much instinctive expressions and the natural environment may serve as a stimulus for the development of certain elements of speech, however much instinctive tendencies, motor and other, may give a predetermined range or mold to linguistic expression. Such human or animal communication, if "communication" it may be called, as is brought about by involuntary, instinctive cries is not, in our sense, language at all.

I have just referred to the "organs of speech," and it would seem at first blush that this is tantamount to an admission that speech itself is an instinctive, biologically predetermined activity. We must not be misled by the mere term. There are, properly speaking, no organs of speech; there are only organs that are incidentally useful in the production of speech sounds. The lungs, the larynx, the palate, the nose, the tongue, the teeth, and the lips, are all so utilized, but they are no more to be thought of as primary organs of speech than are the fingers to be considered as essentially organs of piano-playing or the knees as organs of prayer. Speech is not a simple activity that is carried on by one or more organs biologically adapted to the purpose. It is an extremely complex and ever-shifting network of adjustments—in the brain, in the nervous system, and in the articulating and auditory organs—tending towards the desired end of communication. The lungs developed, roughly speaking, in connection with the necessary biological function known as breathing; the nose, as an organ of smell; the teeth, as organs useful in breaking up food before it was ready for digestion. If, then, these and other organs are being constantly utilized in speech, it is only because any organ, once existent and in so far as it is subject to voluntary control, can be utilized by man for secondary purposes. Physiologically, speech is an overlaid function, or, to be more precise, a group of overlaid functions. It gets what service it can out of organs and functions, nervous and muscular, that have come into being and are maintained for very different ends than its own.

It is true that physiological psychologists speak of the localization of speech in the brain. This can only mean that the sounds of speech are localized in the auditory tract of the brain, or in some circumscribed portion of it, precisely as other classes of sounds are localized; and that the motor processes involved in speech (such as the movements of the glottal cords in the larynx, the movements of the tongue required to pronounce the vowels, lip movements required to articulate certain consonants, and numerous others) are localized in the motor tract precisely as are all other impulses to special motor activities. In the same way control is lodged in the visual tract of the brain over all those processes of visual recognition involved in reading. Naturally the particular points or clusters of points of localization in the several tracts that refer to any element of language are connected in the brain by paths of association, so that the outward, or psycho-physical, aspect of language, is of a vast network of associated localizations in the brain and lower nervous tracts, the auditory localizations being without doubt the most fundamental of all for speech. However, a speechsound localized in the brain, even when associated with the particular movements of the "speech organs" that are required to produce it, is very far from being an element of language. It must be further associated with some element or group of elements of experience, say a visual image or a class of visual images or a feeling of relation, before it has even rudimentary linguistic significance. This "element" of experience is the content or "meaning" of the linguistic unit; the associated auditory, motor, and other cerebral processes that lie immediately back of the act of speaking and the act of hearing speech are merely a complicated symbol of or signal for these "meanings," of which more anon. We see therefore at once that language as such is not and cannot be definitely localized, for it consists of a peculiar symbolic relation—physiologically an arbitrary one—between all possible elements of consciousness on the one hand and certain selected elements localized in the auditory, motor, and other cerebral and nervous tracts on the other. If language can be said to be definitely "localized" in the brain, it is only in that general and rather useless sense in which all aspects of consciousness, all human interest and activity, may be said to be "in the brain." Hence, we have no recourse but to accept language as a fully formed functional system within man's psychic or "spiritual" constitution. We cannot define it as an entity in psycho-physical terms alone, however much the psycho-physical basis is essential to its functioning in the individual.

From the physiologist's or psychologist's point of view we may seem to be making an unwarrantable abstraction in desiring to handle the subject of speech without constant and explicit reference to that basis. However, such an abstraction is justifiable. We can profitably discuss the intention, the form, and the history of speech, precisely as we discuss the nature of any other phase of human culture—say art or religion—as an institutional or cultural entity, leaving the organic and psychological mechanisms back of it as something to be taken for granted. Accordingly, it must be clearly understood that this introduction to the study of speech is not concerned with those aspects of physiology and of physiological psychology that underlie speech. Our study of language is not to be one of the genesis and operation of a concrete mechanism; it is, rather, to be an inquiry into the function and form of the arbitrary systems of symbolism that we term languages.

I have already pointed out that the essence of language consists in the assigning of conventional, voluntarily articulated, sounds, or of their equivalents, to the diverse elements of experience. The word "house" is not a linguistic fact if by it is meant merely the acoustic effect produced on the ear by its constituent consonants and vowels, pronounced in a certain order; nor the motor processes and tactile feelings which make up the articulation of the word; nor the visual perception on the part of the hearer of this articulation; nor the visual perception of the word "house" on the written or printed page; nor the motor processes and tactile feelings which enter into the writing of the word; nor the memory of any or all of these experiences. It is only when these, and possibly still other, associated experiences are automatically associated with the image of a house that they begin to take on the nature of a symbol, a word, an element of language. But the mere fact of such an association is not enough. One might have heard a particular word spoken in an individual house under such impressive circumstances that neither the word nor the image of the house ever recur in consciousness without the other becoming present at the same time. This type of association does not constitute speech. The association must be a purely symbolic one; in other words, the word must denote, tag off, the image, must have no other significance than to serve as a counter to refer to it whenever it is necessary or convenient to do so. Such an association, voluntary and, in a sense, arbitrary as it is, demands a considerable exercise of self-conscious attention. At least to begin with, for habit soon makes the association nearly as automatic as any and more rapid than most.

But we have traveled a little too fast. Were the symbol "house"— whether an auditory, motor, or visual experience or image—attached but to the single image of a particular house once seen, it might perhaps, by an indulgent criticism, be termed an element of speech, yet it is obvious at the outset that speech so constituted would have little or no value for purposes of communication. The world of our experiences must be enormously simplified and generalized before it is possible to make a symbolic inventory of all our experiences of things and relations; and this inventory is imperative before we can convey ideas. The elements of language, the symbols that ticket off experience, must therefore be associated with whole groups, delimited classes, of experience rather than with the single experiences themselves. Only so is communication possible, for the single experience lodges in an individual consciousness and is, strictly speaking, incommunicable. To be communicated it needs to be referred to a class which is tacitly accepted by the community as an identity. Thus, the single impression which I have had of a particular house must be identified with all my other impressions of it. Further, my generalized memory or my "notion" of this house must be merged with the notions that all other individuals who have seen the house have formed of it. The particular experience that we started with has now been widened so as to embrace all possible impressions or images that sentient beings have formed or may form of the house in question. This first simplification of experience is at the bottom of a large number of elements of speech, the so-called proper nouns or names of single individuals or objects. It is, essentially, the type of simplification which underlies, or forms the crude subject of, history and art. But we cannot be content with this measure of reduction of the infinity of experience. We must cut to the bone of things, we must more or less arbitrarily throw whole masses of experience together as similar enough to warrant their being looked upon—mistakenly, but conveniently—as identical. This house and that house and thousands of other phenomena of like character are thought of as having enough in common, in spite of great and obvious differences of detail, to be classed under the same heading. In other words, the speech element "house" is the symbol, first and foremost, not of a single perception, nor even of the notion of a particular object, but of a "concept," in other words, of a convenient capsule of thought that embraces thousands of distinct experiences and that is ready to take in thousands more. If the single significant elements of speech are the symbols of concepts, the actual flow of speech may be interpreted as a record of the setting of these concepts into mutual relations.

The question has often been raised whether thought is possible without speech; further, if speech and thought be not but two facets of the same psychic process. The question is all the more difficult because it has been hedged about by misunderstandings. In the first place, it is well to observe that whether or not thought necessitates symbolism, that is speech, the flow of language itself is not always indicative of thought. We have seen that the typical linguistic element labels a concept. It does not follow from this that the use to which language is put is always or even mainly conceptual. We are not in ordinary life so much concerned with concepts as such as with concrete particularities and specific relations. When I say, for instance, "I had a good breakfast this morning," it is clear that I am not in the throes of laborious thought, that what I have to transmit is hardly more than a pleasurable memory symbolically rendered in the grooves of habitual expression. Each element in the sentence defines a separate concept or conceptual relation or both combined, but the sentence as a whole has no conceptual significance whatever. It is somewhat as though a dynamo capable of generating enough power to run an elevator were operated almost exclusively to feed an electric door-bell. The parallel is more suggestive than at first sight appears. Language may be looked upon as an instrument capable of running a gamut of psychic uses. Its flow not only parallels that of the inner content of consciousness, but parallels it on different levels, ranging from the state of mind that is dominated by particular images to that in which abstract concepts and their relations are alone at the focus of attention and which is ordinarily termed reasoning. Thus the outward form only of language is constant; its inner meaning, its psychic value or intensity, varies freely with attention or the selective interest of the mind, also, needless to say, with the mind's general development. From the point of view of language, thought may be defined as the highest latent or potential content of speech, the content that is obtained by interpreting each of the elements in the flow of language as possessed of its very fullest conceptual value. From this it follows at once that language and thought are not strictly coterminous. At best language can but be the outward facet of thought on the highest, most generalized, level of symbolic expression. To put our viewpoint somewhat differently, language is primarily a pre-rational function. It humbly works up to the thought that is latent in, that may eventually be read into, its classifications and its forms; it is not, as is generally but naïvely assumed, the final label put upon, the finished thought.

Most people, asked if they can think without speech, would probably answer, "Yes, but it is not easy for me to do so. Still I know it can be done." Language is but a garment! But what if language is not so much a garment as a prepared road or groove? It is, indeed, in the highest degree likely that language is an instrument originally put to uses lower than the conceptual plane and that thought arises as a refined interpretation of its content. The product grows, in other words, with the instrument, and thought may be no more conceivable, in its genesis and daily practice, without speech than is mathematical reasoning practicable without the lever of an appropriate mathematical symbolism. No one believes that even the most difficult mathematical proposition is inherently dependent on an arbitrary set of symbols, but it is impossible to suppose that the human mind is capable of arriving at or holding such a proposition without the symbolism. The writer, for one, is strongly of the opinion that the feeling entertained by so many that they can think, or even reason, without language is an illusion. The illusion seems to be due to a number of factors. The simplest of these is the failure to distinguish between imagery and thought. As a matter of fact, no sooner do we try to put an image into conscious relation with another than we find ourselves slipping into a silent flow of words. Thought may be a natural domain apart from the artificial one of speech, but speech would seem to be the only road we know of that leads to it. A still more fruitful source of the illusive feeling that language may be dispensed with in thought is the common failure to realize that language is not identical with its auditory symbolism. The auditory symbolism may be replaced, point for point, by a motor or by a visual symbolism (many people can read, for instance, in a purely visual sense, that is, without the intermediating link of an inner flow of the auditory images that correspond to the printed or written words) or by still other, more subtle and elusive, types of transfer that are not so easy to define. Hence the contention that one thinks without language merely because he is not aware of a coexisting auditory imagery is very far indeed from being a valid one. One may go so far as to suspect that the symbolic expression of thought may in some cases run along outside the fringe of the conscious mind, so that the feeling of a free, nonlinguistic stream of thought is for minds of a certain type a relatively, but only a relatively, justified one. Psycho-physically, this would mean that the auditory or equivalent visual or motor centers in the brain, together with the appropriate paths of association, that are the cerebral equivalent of speech, are touched off so lightly during the process of thought as not to rise into consciousness at all. This would be a limiting case—thought riding lightly on the submerged crests of speech, instead of jogging along with it, hand in hand. The modern psychology has shown us how powerfully symbolism is at work in the unconscious mind. It is therefore easier to understand at the present time than it would have been twenty years ago that the most rarefied thought may be but the conscious counterpart of an unconscious linguistic symbolism.

One word more as to the relation between language and thought. The point of view that we have developed does not by any means preclude the possibility of the growth of speech being in a high degree dependent on the development of thought. We may assume that language arose pre-rationally —just how and on what precise level of mental activity we do not know— but we must not imagine that a highly developed system of speech symbols worked itself out before the genesis of distinct concepts and of thinking, the handling of concepts. We must rather imagine that thought processes set in, as a kind of psychic overflow, almost at the beginning of linguistic expression; further, that the concept, once defined, necessarily reacted on the life of its linguistic symbol, encouraging further linguistic growth. We see this complex process of the interaction of language and thought actually taking place under our eyes. The instrument makes possible the product, the product refines the instrument. The birth of a new concept is invariably foreshadowed by a more or less strained or extended use of old linguistic material; the concept does not attain to individual and independent life until it has found a distinctive linguistic embodiment. In most cases the new symbol is but a thing wrought from linguistic material already in existence in ways mapped out by crushingly despotic precedents. As soon as the word is at hand, we instinctively feel, with something of a sigh of relief, that the concept is ours for the handling. Not until we own the symbol do we feel that we hold a key to the immediate knowledge or understanding of the concept. Would we be so ready to die for "liberty," to struggle for "ideals," if the words themselves were not ringing within us? And the word, as we know, is not only a key; it may also be a fetter.

Language is primarily an auditory system of symbols. In so far as it is articulated it is also a motor system, but the motor aspect of speech is clearly secondary to the auditory. In normal individuals the impulse to speech first takes effect in the sphere of auditory imagery and is then transmitted to the motor nerves that control the organs of speech. The motor processes and the accompanying motor feelings are not, however, the end, the final resting point. They are merely a means and a control leading to auditory perception in both speaker and hearer. Communication, which is the very object of speech, is successfully effected only when the hearer's auditory perceptions are translated into the appropriate and intended flow of imagery or thought or both combined. Hence the cycle of speech, in so far as we may look upon it as a purely external instrument, begins and ends in the realm of sounds. The concordance between the initial auditory imagery and the final auditory perceptions is the social seal or warrant of the successful issue of the process. As we have already seen, the typical course of this process may undergo endless modifications or transfers into equivalent systems without thereby losing its essential formal characteristics.

The most important of these modifications is the abbreviation of the speech process involved in thinking. This has doubtless many forms, according to the structural or functional peculiarities of the individual mind. The least modified form is that known as "talking to one's self" or "thinking aloud." Here the speaker and the hearer are identified in a single person, who may be said to communicate with himself. More significant is the still further abbreviated form in which the sounds of speech are not articulated at all. To this belong all the varieties of silent speech and of normal thinking. The auditory centers alone may be excited; or the impulse to linguistic expression may be communicated as well to the motor nerves that communicate with the organs of speech but be inhibited either in the muscles of these organs or at some point in the motor nerves themselves; or, possibly, the auditory centers may be only slightly, if at all, affected, the speech process manifesting itself directly in the motor sphere. There must be still other types of abbreviation. How common is the excitation of the motor nerves in silent speech, in which no audible or visible articulations result, is shown by the frequent experience of fatigue in the speech organs, particularly in the larynx, after unusually stimulating reading or intensive thinking.

All the modifications so far considered are directly patterned on the typical process of normal speech. Of very great interest and importance is the possibility of transferring the whole system of speech symbolism into other terms than those that are involved in the typical process. This process, as we have seen, is a matter of sounds and of movements intended to produce these sounds. The sense of vision is not brought into play. But let us suppose that one not only hears the articulated sounds but sees the articulations themselves as they are being executed by the speaker. Clearly, if one can only gain a sufficiently high degree of adroitness in perceiving these movements of the speech organs, the way is opened for a new type of speech symbolism—that in which the sound is replaced by the visual image of the articulations that correspond to the sound. This sort of system has no great value for most of us because we are already possessed of the auditory-motor system of which it is at best but an imperfect translation, not all the articulations being visible to the eye. However, it is well known what excellent use deaf-mutes can make of "reading from the lips" as a subsidiary method of apprehending speech. The most important of all visual speech symbolisms is, of course, that of the written or printed word, to which, on the motor side, corresponds the system of delicately adjusted movements which result in the writing or typewriting or other graphic method of recording speech. The significant feature for our recognition in these new types of symbolism, apart from the fact that they are no longer a by-product of normal speech itself, is that each element (letter or written word) in the system corresponds to a specific element (sound or sound-group or spoken word) in the primary system. Written language is thus a point-to-point equivalence, to borrow a mathematical phrase, to its spoken counterpart. The written forms are secondary symbols of the spoken ones—symbols of symbols—yet so close is the correspondence that they may, not only in theory but in the actual practice of certain eye-readers and, possibly, in certain types of thinking, be entirely substituted for the spoken ones. Yet the auditory-motor associations are probably always latent at the least, that is, they are unconsciously brought into play. Even those who read and think without the slightest use of sound imagery are, at last analysis, dependent on it. They are merely handling the circulating medium, the money, of visual symbols as a convenient substitute for the economic goods and services of the fundamental auditory symbols.

The possibilities of linguistic transfer are practically unlimited. A familiar example is the Morse telegraph code, in which the letters of written speech are represented by a conventionally fixed sequence of longer or shorter ticks. Here the transfer takes place from the written word rather than directly from the sounds of spoken speech. The letter of the telegraph code is thus a symbol of a symbol of a symbol. It does not, of course, in the least follow that the skilled operator, in order to arrive at an understanding of a telegraphic message, needs to transpose the individual sequence of ticks into a visual image of the word before he experiences its normal auditory image. The precise method of reading off speech from the telegraphic communication undoubtedly varies widely with the individual. It is even conceivable, if not exactly likely, that certain operators may have learned to think directly, so far as the purely conscious part of the process of thought is concerned, in terms of the tick-auditory symbolism or, if they happen to have a strong natural bent toward motor symbolism, in terms of the correlated tactile-motor symbolism developed in the sending of telegraphic messages.

Still another interesting group of transfers are the different gesture languages, developed for the use of deaf-mutes, of Trappist monks vowed to perpetual silence, or of communicating parties that are within seeing distance of each other but are out of earshot. Some of these systems are one-to-one equivalences of the normal system of speech; others, like military gesture-symbolism or the gesture language of the Plains Indians of North America (understood by tribes of mutually unintelligible forms of speech) are imperfect transfers, limiting themselves to the rendering of such grosser speech elements as are an imperative minimum under difficult circumstances. In these latter systems, as in such still more imperfect symbolisms as those used at sea or in the woods, it may be contended that language no longer properly plays a part but that the ideas are directly conveyed by an utterly unrelated symbolic process or by a quasi-instinctive imitativeness. Such an interpretation would be erroneous. The intelligibility of these vaguer symbolisms can hardly be due to anything but their automatic and silent translation into the terms of a fuller flow of speech.

We shall no doubt conclude that all voluntary communication of ideas, aside from normal speech, is either a transfer, direct or indirect, from the typical symbolism of language as spoken and heard or, at the least, involves the intermediary of truly linguistic symbolism. This is a fact of the highest importance. Auditory imagery and the correlated motor imagery leading to articulation are, by whatever devious ways we follow the process, the historic fountain-head of all speech and of all thinking. One other point is of still greater importance. The ease with which speech symbolism can be transferred from one sense to another, from technique to technique, itself indicates that the mere sounds of speech are not the essential fact of language, which lies rather in the classification, in the formal patterning, and in the relating of concepts. Once more, language, as a structure, is on its inner face the mold of thought. It is this abstracted language, rather more than the physical facts of speech, that is to concern us in our inquiry.

There is no more striking general fact about language than its universality. One may argue as to whether a particular tribe engages in activities that are worthy of the name of religion or of art, but we know of no people that is not possessed of a fully developed language. The lowliest South African Bushman speaks in the forms of a rich symbolic system that is in essence perfectly comparable to the speech of the cultivated Frenchman. It goes without saying that the more abstract concepts are not nearly so plentifully represented in the language of the savage, nor is there the rich terminology and the finer definition of nuances that reflect the higher culture. Yet the sort of linguistic development that parallels the historic growth of culture and which, in its later stages, we associate with literature is, at best, but a superficial thing. The fundamental groundwork of language—the development of a clear-cut phonetic system, the specific association of speech elements with concepts, and the delicate provision for the formal expression of all manner of relations—all this meets us rigidly perfected and systematized in every language known to us. Many primitive languages have a formal richness, a latent luxuriance of expression, that eclipses anything known to the languages of modern civilization. Even in the mere matter of the inventory of speech the layman must be prepared for strange surprises. Popular statements as to the extreme poverty of expression to which primitive languages are doomed are simply myths. Scarcely less impressive than the universality of speech is its almost incredible diversity. Those of us that have studied French or German, or, better yet, Latin or Greek, know in what varied forms a thought may run. The formal divergences between the English plan and the Latin plan, however, are comparatively slight in the perspective of what we know of more exotic linguistic patterns. The universality and the diversity of speech lead to a significant inference. We are forced to believe that language is an immensely ancient heritage of the human race, whether or not all forms of speech are the historical outgrowth of a single pristine form. It is doubtful if any other cultural asset of man, be it the art of drilling for fire or of chipping stone, may lay claim to a greater age. I am inclined to believe that it antedated even the lowliest developments of material culture, that these developments, in fact, were not strictly possible until language, the tool of significant expression, had itself taken shape.

The Elements of Speech

We have more than once referred to the "elements of speech," by which we understood, roughly speaking, what are ordinarily called "words." We must now look more closely at these elements and acquaint ourselves with the stuff of language. The very simplest element of speech—and by "speech" we shall hence-forth mean the auditory system of speech symbolism, the flow of spoken words—is the individual sound, though, as we shall see later on, the sound is not itself a simple structure but the resultant of a series of independent, yet closely correlated, adjustments in the organs of speech. And yet the individual sound is not, properly considered, an element of speech at all, for speech is a significant function and the sound as such has no significance. It happens occasionally that the single sound is an independently significant element (such as French *a* "has" and *à* "to" or Latin *i* "go!"), but such cases are fortuitous coincidences between individual sound and significant word. The coincidence is apt to be fortuitous not only in theory but in point of actual historic fact; thus, the instances cited are merely reduced forms of originally fuller phonetic groups—Latin *habet* and *ad* and Indo-European *ei* respectively. If language is a structure and if the significant elements of language are the bricks of the structure, then the sounds of speech can only be compared to the unformed and unburnt clay of which the bricks are fashioned. In this chapter we shall have nothing further to do with sounds as sounds.

The true, significant elements of language are generally sequences of sounds that are either words, significant parts of words, or word groupings. What distinguishes each of these elements is that it is the outward sign of a specific idea, whether of a single concept or image or of a number of such concepts or images definitely connected into a whole. The single word may or may not be the simplest significant element we have to deal with. The English words *sing, sings, singing, singer* each conveys a perfectly definite and intelligible idea, though the idea is disconnected and is therefore functionally of no practical value. We recognize immediately that these words are of two sorts. The first word, *sing*, is an indivisible phonetic entity conveying the notion of a certain specific activity. The other words all involve the same fundamental notion but, owing to the addition of other phonetic elements, this notion is given a particular twist that modifies or more closely defines it. They represent, in a sense, compounded concepts that have flowered from the fundamental one. We may, therefore, analyze the words *sings*, *singing*, and *singer* as binary expressions involving a fundamental concept, a concept of subject matter (*sing*), and a further concept of more abstract order—one of person, number, time, condition, function, or of several of these combined.

If we symbolize such a term as *sing* by the algebraic formula A, we shall have to symbolize such terms as *sings* and *singer* by the formula A + b. [1] The element A may be either a complete and independent word (*sing*) or the fundamental substance, the so-called root or stem [2] or "radical element" (*sing-*) of a word. The element b (*-s, -ing, -er*) is the indicator of a subsidiary and, as a rule, a more abstract concept; in the widest sense of the word "form," it puts upon the fundamental concept a formal limitation. We may term it a "grammatical element" or affix. As we shall see later on, the grammatical element or the grammatical increment, as we had better put it, need not be suffixed to the radical element. It may be a prefixed element (like the *un-* of *unsingable*), it may be inserted into the very body of the stem (like the *n* of the Latin *vinco* "I conquer" as contrasted with its absence in *vici* "I have conquered"), it may be the complete or partial repetition of the stem, or it may consist of some modification of the inner form of the stem (change of vowel, as in *sung* and *song*; change of consonant as in *dead* and *death*; change of accent; actual abbreviation). Each and every one of these types of grammatical element or modification has this peculiarity, that it may not, in the vast majority of cases, be used independently but needs to be somehow attached to or welded with a radical element in order to convey an intelligible notion. We had better, therefore, modify our formula, A + b, to A + (b), the round brackets symbolizing the incapacity of an element to stand alone. The grammatical element, moreover, is not only non-existent except as associated with a radical one, it does not even, as a rule, obtain its measure of significance unless it is associated with a particular class of radical elements. Thus, the *-s* of English *he hits* symbolizes an utterly different notion from the *-s* of *books*, merely because *hit* and *book* are differently classified as to function. We must hasten to observe, however, that while the radical element may, on occasion, be identical with the word, it does not follow that it may always, or even customarily, be used as a word. Thus, the *hort-* "garden" of such Latin forms as *hortus, horti,* and *horto* is as much of an abstraction, though one yielding a more easily apprehended significance, than the *-ing* of *singing*. Neither exists as an independently intelligible and satisfying element of speech. Both the radical element, as such, and the grammatical element, therefore, are reached only by a process of abstraction. It seemed proper to symbolize *sing-er* as A + (b); *hort-us* must be symbolized as (A) + (b).

So far, the first speech element that we have found which we can say actually "exists" is the word. Before defining the word, however, we must look a little more closely at the type of word that is illustrated by *sing*. Are we, after all, justified in identifying it with a radical element? Does it represent a simple correspondence between concept and linguistic expression? Is the element *sing-*, that we have abstracted from *sings, singing,* and *singer* and to which we may justly ascribe a general unmodified conceptual value, actually the same linguistic fact as the word *sing*? It would almost seem absurd to doubt it, yet a little reflection only is needed to convince us that the doubt is entirely legitimate. The word *sing* cannot, as a matter of fact, be freely used to refer to its own conceptual content. The existence of such evidently related forms as *sang* and *sung* at once shows that it cannot refer to past time, but that, for at least an important part of its range of usage, it is limited to the present. On the other hand, the use of *sing* as an "infinitive" (in such locutions as *to sing* and *he will sing*) does indicate that there is a fairly strong tendency for the word *sing* to represent the full, untrammeled amplitude of a specific concept. Yet if *sing* were, in any adequate sense, the fixed expression of the unmodified concept, there should be no room for such vocalic aberrations as we find in *sang* and *sung* and *song,* nor should we find *sing* specifically used to indicate present time for all persons but one (third person singular *sings*).

The truth of the matter is that *sing* is a kind of twilight word, trembling between the status of a true radical element and that of a modified word of the type of *singing*. Though it has no outward sign to indicate that it conveys more than a generalized idea, we do feel that there hangs about it a variable mist of added value. The formula A does not seem to represent it so well as A + (0). We might suspect *sing* of belonging to the A + (b) type, with the reservation that the (b) had vanished. This report of the "feel" of the word is far from fanciful, for historical evidence does, in all earnest, show that *sing* is in origin a number of quite distinct words, of type A + (b), that have pooled their separate values. The (b) of each of these has gone as a tangible phonetic element; its force, however, lingers on in weakened measure. The *sing* of *I sing* is the correspondent of the Anglo-Saxon *singe*; the infinitive *sing*, of *singan*; the imperative *sing* of *sing*. Ever since the breakdown of English forms that set in about the time of the Norman Conquest, our language has been straining towards the creation of simple concept-words, unalloyed by formal connotations, but it has not yet succeeded in this, apart, possibly, from isolated adverbs and other elements of that sort. Were the typical unanalyzable word of the language truly a pure concept-word (type A) instead of being of a strangely transitional type (type A + [0]), our *sing* and *work* and *house* and thousands of others would compare with the genuine radical-words of numerous other languages. [3] Such a radical-word, to take a random example, is the Nootka [4] word *hamot* "bone." Our English correspondent is only superficially comparable. *Hamot* means "bone" in a quite indefinite sense; to our English word clings the notion of singularity. The Nootka Indian can convey the idea of plurality, in one of several ways, if he so desires, but he does not need to; *hamot* may do for either singular or plural, should no interest happen to attach to the distinction. As soon as we say "bone" (aside from its secondary usage to indicate material), we not merely specify the nature of the object but we imply, whether we will or no, that there is but one of these objects to be considered. And this increment of value makes all the difference.

We now know of four distinct formal types of word: A (Nootka *hamot*); A + (0) (*sing, bone*); A + (b) (*singing*); (A) + (b) (Latin *hortus*). There is but one other type that is fundamentally possible: A + B, the union of two (or more) independently occurring radical elements into a single term. Such a word is the compound *fire-engine* or a Sioux form equivalent to *eat-stand* (i.e., "to eat while standing"). It frequently happens, however, that one of the radical elements becomes functionally so subordinated to the other that it takes on the character of a grammatical element. We may symbolize this by A + b, a type that may gradually, by loss of external connection between the subordinated element b and its independent counterpart B merge with the commoner type A + (b). A word like *beautiful* is an example of A + b, the -*ful* barely preserving the impress of its lineage. A word like *homely*, on the other hand, is clearly of the type A + (b), for no one but a linguistic student is aware of the connection between the -*ly* and the independent word *like*.

In actual use, of course, these five (or six) fundamental types may be indefinitely complicated in a number of ways. The (0) may have a multiple value; in other words, the inherent formal modification of the basic notion of the word may affect more than one category. In such a Latin word as *cor* "heart," for instance, not only is a concrete concept conveyed, but there cling to the form, which is actually shorter than its own radical element (*cord-*), the three distinct, yet intertwined, formal concepts of singularity, gender classification (neuter), and case (subjective-objective). The complete grammatical formula for *cor* is, then, A + (0) + (0) + (0), though the merely external, phonetic formula would be (A)—, (A) indicating the abstracted "stem" *cord-*, the minus sign a loss of material. The significant thing about such a word as *cor* is that the three conceptual limitations are not merely expressed by implication as the word sinks into place in a sentence; they are tied up, for good and all, within the very vitals of the word and cannot be eliminated by any possibility of usage.

Other complications result from a manifolding of parts. In a given word there may be several elements of the order A (we have already symbolized this by the type A + B), of the order (A), of the order b, and of the order (b). Finally, the various types may be combined among themselves in endless ways. A comparatively simple language like English, or even Latin, illustrates but a modest proportion of these theoretical possibilities. But if we take our examples freely from the vast storehouse of language, from languages exotic as well as from those that we are more familiar with, we shall find that there is hardly a possibility that is not realized in actual usage. One example will do for thousands, one complex type for hundreds of possible types. I select it from Paiute, the language of the Indians of the arid plateaus of southwestern Utah. The word *wii-to-kuchum-punku-rügani-yugwi-va-ntü-m(ü)*[5] is of unusual length even for its own language, but it is no psychological monster for all that. It means "they who are going to sit and cut up with a knife a black cow (*or* bull)," or, in the order of the Indian elements, "knife-black-buffalo-pet-cut up-sit(plur.)-future-participle-animate plur." The formula for this word, in accordance with our symbolism, would be

(F) + (E) + C + d + A + B + (g) + (h) + (i) + (0). It is the plural of the future participle of a compound verb "to sit and cut up"—A + B. The elements (g) —which denotes futurity—, (h)—a participial suffix—, and (i)—indicating the animate plural—are grammatical elements which convey nothing when detached. The formula (0) is intended to imply that the finished word conveys, in addition to what is definitely expressed, a further relational idea, that of subjectivity; in other words, the form can only be used as the subject of a sentence, not in an objective or other syntactic relation. The radical element A ("to cut up"), before entering into combination with the coördinate element B ("to sit"), is itself compounded with two nominal elements or element-groups—an instrumentally used stem (F) ("knife"), which may be freely used as the radical element of noun forms but cannot be employed as an absolute noun in its given form, and an objectively used group—(E) + C + d ("black cow *or* bull"). This group in turn consists of an adjectival radical element (E) ("black"), which cannot be independently employed (the absolute notion of "black" can be rendered only as the participle of a verb: "black-be-ing"), and the compound noun C + d ("buffalo-pet"). The radical element C properly means "buffalo," but the element d, properly an independently occurring noun meaning "horse" (originally "dog" or "domesticated animal" in general), is regularly used as a quasi-subordinate element indicating that the animal denoted by the stem to which it is affixed is owned by a human being. It will be observed that the whole complex (F) + (E) + C + d + A + B is functionally no more than a verbal base, corresponding to the *sing-* of an English form like *singing*; that this complex remains verbal in force on the addition of the temporal element (g)—this (g), by the way, must not be understood as appended to B alone, but to the whole basic complex as a unit—; and that the elements (h) + (i) + (0) transform the verbal expression into a formally well-defined noun.

It is high time that we decided just what is meant by a word. Our first impulse, no doubt, would have been to define the word as the symbolic, linguistic counterpart of a single concept. We now know that such a definition is impossible. In truth it is impossible to define the word from a functional standpoint at all, for the word may be anything from the expression of a single concept—concrete or abstract or purely relational (as in *of* or *by* or *and*)—to the expression of a complete thought (as in Latin *dico* "I say" or, with greater elaborateness of form, in a Nootka verb form denoting "I have been accustomed to eat twenty round objects [e.g., apples] while engaged in [doing so and so]"). In the latter case the word becomes identical with the sentence. The word is merely a form, a definitely molded entity that takes in as much or as little of the conceptual material of the whole thought as the genius of the language cares to allow. Thus it is that while the single radical elements and grammatical elements, the carriers of isolated concepts, are comparable as we pass from language to language, the finished words are not. Radical (or grammatical) element and sentence —these are the primary *functional* units of speech, the former as an abstracted minimum, the latter as the esthetically satisfying embodiment of a unified thought. The actual *formal* units of speech, the words, may on occasion identify themselves with either of the two functional units; more often they mediate between the two extremes, embodying one or more radical notions and also one or more subsidiary ones. We may put the whole matter in a nutshell by saying that the radical and grammatical elements of language, abstracted as they are from the realities of speech, respond to the conceptual world of science, abstracted as it is from the realities of experience, and that the word, the existent unit of living speech, responds to the unit of actually apprehended experience, of history, of art. The sentence is the logical counterpart of the complete thought only if it be felt as made up of the radical and grammatical elements that lurk in the recesses of its words. It is the psychological counterpart of experience, of art, when it is felt, as indeed it normally is, as the finished play of word with word. As the necessity of defining thought solely and exclusively for its own sake becomes more urgent, the word becomes increasingly irrelevant as a means. We can therefore easily understand why the mathematician and the symbolic logician are driven to discard the word and to build up their thought with the help of symbols which have, each of them, a rigidly unitary value.

But is not the word, one may object, as much of an abstraction as the radical element? Is it not as arbitrarily lifted out of the living sentence as is the minimum conceptual element out of the word? Some students of language have, indeed, looked upon the word as such an abstraction, though with very doubtful warrant, it seems to me. It is true that in particular cases, especially in some of the highly synthetic languages of aboriginal America, it is not always easy to say whether a particular element of language is to be interpreted as an independent word or as part of a larger word. These transitional cases, puzzling as they may be on occasion, do not, however, materially weaken the case for the psychological validity of the word. Linguistic experience, both as expressed in standardized, written form and as tested in daily usage, indicates overwhelmingly that there is not, as a rule, the slightest difficulty in bringing the word to consciousness as a psychological reality. No more convincing test could be desired than this, that the naïve Indian, quite unaccustomed to the concept of the written word, has nevertheless no serious difficulty in dictating a text to a linguistic student word by word; he tends, of course, to run his words together as in actual speech, but if he is called to a halt and is made to understand what is desired, he can readily isolate the words as such, repeating them as units. He regularly refuses, on the other hand, to isolate the radical or grammatical element, on the ground that it "makes no sense." [[6]] What, then, is the objective criterion of the word? The speaker and hearer feel the word, let us grant, but how shall we justify their feeling? If function is not the ultimate criterion of the word, what is?

It is easier to ask the question than to answer it. The best that we can do is to say that the word is one of the smallest, completely satisfying bits of isolated "meaning" into which the sentence resolves itself. It cannot be cut into without a disturbance of meaning, one or the other or both of the severed parts remaining as a helpless waif on our hands. In practice this unpretentious criterion does better service than might be supposed. In such a sentence as *It is unthinkable*, it is simply impossible to group the elements into any other and smaller "words" than the three indicated. *Think* or *thinkable* might be isolated, but as neither *un-* nor *-able* nor *is-un* yields a measurable satisfaction, we are compelled to leave *unthinkable* as an integral whole, a miniature bit of art. Added to the "feel" of the word are frequently, but by no means invariably, certain external phonetic characteristics. Chief of these is accent. In many, perhaps in most, languages the single word is marked by a unifying accent, an emphasis on one of the syllables, to which the rest are subordinated. The particular syllable that is to be so distinguished is dependent, needless to say, on the special genius of the language. The importance of accent as a unifying feature of the word is obvious in such English examples as *unthinkable, characterizing*. The long Paiute word that we have analyzed is marked as a rigid phonetic unit by several features, chief of which are the accent on its second syllable (*wii'*-"knife") and the slurring ("unvoicing," to use the technical phonetic term) of its final vowel (-*mü*, animate plural). Such features as accent, cadence, and the treatment of consonants and vowels within the body of a word are often useful as aids in the external demarcation of the word, but they must by no means be interpreted, as is sometimes done, as themselves responsible for its psychological existence. They at best but strengthen a feeling of unity that is already present on other grounds.

We have already seen that the major functional unit of speech, the sentence, has, like the word, a psychological as well as a merely logical or abstracted existence. Its definition is not difficult. It is the linguistic expression of a proposition. It combines a subject of discourse with a statement in regard to this subject. Subject and "predicate" may be combined in a single word, as in Latin *dico*; each may be expressed independently, as in the English equivalent, *I say*; each or either may be so qualified as to lead to complex propositions of many sorts. No matter how many of these qualifying elements (words or functional parts of words) are introduced, the sentence does not lose its feeling of unity so long as each and every one of them falls in place as contributory to the definition of either the subject of discourse or the core of the predicate [7]. Such a sentence as *The mayor of New York is going to deliver a speech of welcome in French* is readily felt as a unified statement, incapable of reduction by the transfer of certain of its elements, in their given form, to the preceding or following sentences. The contributory ideas of *of New York*, *of welcome*, and *in French* may be eliminated without hurting the idiomatic flow of the sentence. *The mayor is going to deliver a speech* is a perfectly intelligible proposition. But further than this we cannot go in the process of reduction. We cannot say, for instance, *Mayor is going to deliver*.[8] The reduced sentence resolves itself into the subject of discourse—*the mayor*—and the predicate—*is going to deliver a speech*. It is customary to say that the true subject of such a sentence is *mayor*, the true predicate *is going* or even *is*, the other elements being strictly subordinate. Such an analysis, however, is purely schematic and is without psychological value. It is much better frankly to recognize the fact that either or both of the two terms of the sentence-proposition may be incapable of expression in the form of single words. There are languages that can convey all that is conveyed by *The-mayor is-going-to-deliver-a-speech* in two words, a subject word and a predicate word, but English is not so highly synthetic. The point that we are really making here is that underlying the finished sentence is a living sentence type, of fixed formal characteristics. These fixed types or actual sentence-groundworks may be freely overlaid by such additional matter as the speaker or writer cares to put on, but they are themselves as rigidly "given" by tradition as are the radical and grammatical elements abstracted from the finished word. New words may be consciously created from these fundamental elements on the analogy of old ones, but hardly new types of words. In the same way new sentences are being constantly created, but always on strictly traditional lines. The enlarged sentence, however, allows as a rule of considerable freedom in the handling of what may be called "unessential" parts. It is this margin of freedom which gives us the opportunity of individual style.

The habitual association of radical elements, grammatical elements, words, and sentences with concepts or groups of concepts related into wholes is the fact itself of language. It is important to note that there is in all languages a certain randomness of association. Thus, the idea of "hide" may be also expressed by the word "conceal," the notion of "three times" also by "thrice." The multiple expression of a single concept is universally felt as a source of linguistic strength and variety, not as a needless extravagance. More irksome is a random correspondence between idea and linguistic expression in the field of abstract and relational concepts, particularly when the concept is embodied in a grammatical element. Thus, the randomness of the expression of plurality in such words as *books*, *oxen*, *sheep*, and *geese* is felt to be rather more, I fancy, an unavoidable and traditional predicament than a welcome luxuriance. It is obvious that a language cannot go beyond a certain point in this randomness. Many languages go incredibly far in this respect, it is true, but linguistic history shows conclusively that sooner or later the less frequently occurring associations are ironed out at the expense of the more vital ones. In other words, all languages have an inherent tendency to economy of expression. Were this tendency entirely inoperative, there would be no grammar. The fact of grammar, a universal trait of language, is simply a generalized expression of the feeling that analogous concepts and relations are most conveniently symbolized in analogous forms. Were a language ever completely "grammatical," it would be a perfect engine of conceptual expression. Unfortunately, or luckily, no language is tyrannically consistent. All grammars leak.

Up to the present we have been assuming that the material of language reflects merely the world of concepts and, on what I have ventured to call the "pre-rational" plane, of images, which are the raw material of concepts. We have, in other words, been assuming that language moves entirely in the ideational or cognitive sphere. It is time that we amplified the picture. The volitional aspect of consciousness also is to some extent explicitly provided for in language. Nearly all languages have special means for the expression of commands (in the imperative forms of the verb, for example) and of desires, unattained or unattainable (*Would he might come!* or *Would he were here!*) The emotions, on the whole, seem to be given a less adequate outlet. Emotion, indeed, is proverbially inclined to speechlessness. Most, if not all, the interjections are to be put to the credit of emotional expression, also, it may be, a number of linguistic elements expressing certain modalities, such as dubitative or potential forms, which may be interpreted as reflecting the emotional states of hesitation or doubt—attenuated fear. On the whole, it must be admitted that ideation reigns supreme in language, that volition and emotion come in as distinctly secondary factors. This, after all, is perfectly intelligible. The world of image and concept, the endless and ever-shifting picture of objective reality, is the unavoidable subject-matter of human communication, for it is only, or mainly, in terms of this world that effective action is possible. Desire, purpose, emotion are the personal color of the objective world; they are applied privately by the individual soul and are of relatively little importance to the neighboring one. All this does not mean that volition and emotion are not expressed. They are, strictly speaking, never absent from normal speech, but their expression is not of a truly linguistic nature. The nuances of emphasis, tone, and phrasing, the varying speed and continuity of utterance, the accompanying bodily movements, all these express something of the inner life of impulse and feeling, but as these means of expression are, at last analysis, but modified forms of the instinctive utterance that man shares with the lower animals, they cannot be considered as forming part of the essential cultural conception of language, however much they may be inseparable from its actual life. And this instinctive expression of volition and emotion is, for the most part, sufficient, often more than sufficient, for the purposes of communication.

There are, it is true, certain writers on the psychology of language [9] who deny its prevailingly cognitive character but attempt, on the contrary, to demonstrate the origin of most linguistic elements within the domain of feeling. I confess that I am utterly unable to follow them. What there is of truth in their contentions may be summed up, it seems to me, by saying that most words, like practically all elements of consciousness, have an associated feeling-tone, a mild, yet none the less real and at times insidiously powerful, derivative of pleasure or pain. This feeling-tone, however, is not as a rule an inherent value in the word itself; it is rather a sentimental growth on the word's true body, on its conceptual kernel. Not only may the feeling-tone change from one age to another (this, of course, is true of the conceptual content as well), but it varies remarkably from individual to individual according to the personal associations of each, varies, indeed, from time to time in a single individual's consciousness as his experiences mold him and his moods change. To be sure, there are socially accepted feeling-tones, or ranges of feeling-tone, for many words over and above the force of individual association, but they are exceedingly variable and elusive things at best. They rarely have the rigidity of the central, primary fact. We all grant, for instance, that *storm*, *tempest*, and *hurricane*, quite aside from their slight differences of actual meaning, have distinct feeling-tones, tones that are felt by all sensitive speakers and readers of English in a roughly equivalent fashion. *Storm*, we feel, is a more general and a decidedly less "magnificent" word than the other two; *tempest* is not only associated with the sea but is likely, in the minds of many, to have obtained a softened glamour from a specific association with Shakespeare's great play; *hurricane* has a greater forthrightness, a directer ruthlessness than its synonyms. Yet the individual's feeling-tones for these words are likely to vary enormously. To some *tempest* and *hurricane* may seem "soft," literary words, the simpler *storm* having a fresh, rugged value which the others do not possess (think of *storm and stress*). If we have browsed much in our childhood days in books of the Spanish Main, *hurricane* is likely to have a pleasurably bracing tone; if we have had the misfortune to be caught in one, we are not unlikely to feel the word as cold, cheerless, sinister.

    The feeling-tones of words are of no use, strictly speaking, to science; the philosopher, if he desires to arrive at truth rather than merely to persuade, finds them his most insidious enemies. But man is rarely engaged in pure science, in solid thinking. Generally his mental activities are bathed in a warm current of feeling and he seizes upon the feeling-tones of words as gentle aids to the desired excitation. They are naturally of great value to the literary artist. It is interesting to note, however, that even to the artist they are a danger. A word whose customary feeling-tone is too unquestioningly accepted becomes a plushy bit of furniture, a *cliché*. Every now and then the artist has to fight the feeling-tone, to get the word to mean what it nakedly and conceptually should mean, depending for the effect of feeling on the creative power of an individual juxtaposition of concepts or images.

III

The Sounds of Language

We have seen that the mere phonetic framework of speech does not constitute the inner fact of language and that the single sound of articulated speech is not, as such, a linguistic element at all. For all that, speech is so inevitably bound up with sounds and their articulation that we can hardly avoid giving the subject of phonetics some general consideration. Experience has shown that neither the purely formal aspects of a language nor the course of its history can be fully understood without reference to the sounds in which this form and this history are embodied. A detailed survey of phonetics would be both too technical for the general reader and too loosely related to our main theme to warrant the needed space, but we can well afford to consider a few outstanding facts and ideas connected with the sounds of language.

The feeling that the average speaker has of his language is that it is built up, acoustically speaking, of a comparatively small number of distinct sounds, each of which is rather accurately provided for in the current alphabet by one letter or, in a few cases, by two or more alternative letters. As for the languages of foreigners, he generally feels that, aside from a few striking differences that cannot escape even the uncritical ear, the sounds they use are the same as those he is familiar with but that there is a mysterious "accent" to these foreign languages, a certain unanalyzed phonetic character, apart from the sounds as such, that gives them their air of strangeness. This naïve feeling is largely illusory on both scores. Phonetic analysis convinces one that the number of clearly distinguishable sounds and nuances of sounds that are habitually employed by the speakers of a language is far greater than they themselves recognize. Probably not one English speaker out of a hundred has the remotest idea that the *t* of a word like *sting* is not at all the same sound as the *t* of *teem*, the latter *t* having a fullness of "breath release" that is inhibited in the former case by the preceding *s*; that the *ea* of *meat* is of perceptibly shorter duration than the *ea* of *mead*; or that the final *s* of a word like *heads* is not the full, buzzing *z* sound of the *s* in such a word as *please*. It is the frequent failure of foreigners, who have acquired a practical mastery of English and who have eliminated all the cruder phonetic shortcomings of their less careful brethren, to observe such minor distinctions that helps to give their English pronunciation the curiously elusive "accent" that we all vaguely feel. We do not diagnose the "accent" as the total acoustic effect produced by a series of slight but specific phonetic errors for the very good reason that we have never made clear to ourselves our own phonetic stock in trade. If two languages taken at random, say English and Russian, are compared as to their phonetic systems, we are more apt than not to find that very few of the phonetic elements of the one find an exact analogue in the other. Thus, the *t* of a Russian word like *tam* "there" is neither the English *t* of *sting* nor the English *t* of *teem*. It differs from both in its "dental" articulation, in other words, in being produced by contact of the tip of the tongue with the upper teeth, not, as in English, by contact of the tongue back of the tip with the gum ridge above the teeth; moreover, it differs from the *t* of *teem* also in the absence of a marked "breath release" before the following vowel is attached, so that its acoustic effect is of a more precise, "metallic" nature than in English. Again, the English *l* is unknown in Russian, which possesses, on the other hand, two distinct *l*-sounds that the normal English speaker would find it difficult exactly to reproduce—a "hollow," guttural-like *l* and a "soft," palatalized *l*-sound that is only very approximately rendered, in English terms, as *ly*. Even so simple and, one would imagine, so invariable a sound as *m* differs in the two languages. In a Russian word like *most* "bridge" the *m* is not the same as the *m* of the English word *most*; the lips are more fully rounded during its articulation, so that it makes a heavier, more resonant impression on the ear. The vowels, needless to say, differ completely in English and Russian, hardly any two of them being quite the same.

I have gone into these illustrative details, which are of little or no specific interest for us, merely in order to provide something of an experimental basis to convince ourselves of the tremendous variability of speech sounds. Yet a complete inventory of the acoustic resources of all the European languages, the languages nearer home, while unexpectedly large, would still fall far short of conveying a just idea of the true range of human articulation. In many of the languages of Asia, Africa, and aboriginal America there are whole classes of sounds that most of us have no knowledge of. They are not necessarily more difficult of enunciation than sounds more familiar to our ears; they merely involve such muscular adjustments of the organs of speech as we have never habituated ourselves to. It may be safely said that the total number of possible sounds is greatly in excess of those actually in use. Indeed, an experienced phonetician should have no difficulty in inventing sounds that are unknown to objective investigation. One reason why we find it difficult to believe that the range of possible speech sounds is indefinitely large is our habit of conceiving the sound as a simple, unanalyzable impression instead of as the resultant of a number of distinct muscular adjustments that take place simultaneously. A slight change in any one of these adjustments gives us a new sound which is akin to the old one, because of the continuance of the other adjustments, but which is acoustically distinct from it, so sensitive has the human ear become to the nuanced play of the vocal mechanism. Another reason for our lack of phonetic imagination is the fact that, while our ear is delicately responsive to the sounds of speech, the muscles of our speech organs have early in life become exclusively accustomed to the particular adjustments and systems of adjustment that are required to produce the traditional sounds of the language. All or nearly all other adjustments have become permanently inhibited, whether through inexperience or through gradual elimination. Of course the power to produce these inhibited adjustments is not entirely lost, but the extreme difficulty we experience in learning the new sounds of foreign languages is sufficient evidence of the strange rigidity that has set in for most people in the voluntary control of the speech organs. The point may be brought home by contrasting the comparative lack of freedom of voluntary speech movements with the all but perfect freedom of voluntary gesture.[10] Our rigidity in articulation is the price we have had to pay for easy mastery of a highly necessary symbolism. One cannot be both splendidly free in the random choice of movements and selective with deadly certainty.[11]

There are, then, an indefinitely large number of articulated sounds available for the mechanics of speech; any given language makes use of an explicit, rigidly economical selection of these rich resources; and each of the many possible sounds of speech is conditioned by a number of independent muscular adjustments that work together simultaneously towards its production. A full account of the activity of each of the organs of speech—in so far as its activity has a bearing on language—is impossible here, nor can we concern ourselves in a systematic way with the classification of sounds on the basis of their mechanics.[12] A few bold outlines are all that we can attempt. The organs of speech are the lungs and bronchial tubes; the throat, particularly that part of it which is known as the larynx or, in popular parlance, the "Adam's apple"; the nose; the uvula, which is the soft, pointed, and easily movable organ that depends from the rear of the palate; the palate, which is divided into a posterior, movable "soft palate" or velum and a "hard palate"; the tongue; the teeth; and the lips. The palate, lower palate, tongue, teeth, and lips may be looked upon as a combined resonance chamber, whose constantly varying shape, chiefly due to the extreme mobility of the tongue, is the main factor in giving the outgoing breath its precise quality [13] of sound.

The lungs and bronchial tubes are organs of speech only in so far as they supply and conduct the current of outgoing air without which audible articulation is impossible. They are not responsible for any specific sound or acoustic feature of sounds except, possibly, accent or stress. It may be that differences of stress are due to slight differences in the contracting force of the lung muscles, but even this influence of the lungs is denied by some students, who explain the fluctuations of stress that do so much to color speech by reference to the more delicate activity of the glottal cords. These glottal cords are two small, nearly horizontal, and highly sensitive membranes within the larynx, which consists, for the most part, of two large and several smaller cartilages and of a number of small muscles that control the action of the cords.

The cords, which are attached to the cartilages, are to the human speech organs what the two vibrating reeds are to a clarinet or the strings to a violin. They are capable of at least three distinct types of movement, each of which is of the greatest importance for speech. They may be drawn towards or away from each other, they may vibrate like reeds or strings, and they may become lax or tense in the direction of their length. The last class of these movements allows the cords to vibrate at different "lengths" or degrees of tenseness and is responsible for the variations in pitch which are present not only in song but in the more elusive modulations of ordinary speech. The two other types of glottal action determine the nature of the voice, "voice" being a convenient term for breath as utilized in speech. If the cords are well apart, allowing the breath to escape in unmodified form, we have the condition technically known as "voicelessness." All sounds produced under these circumstances are "voiceless" sounds. Such are the simple, unmodified breath as it passes into the mouth, which is, at least approximately, the same as the sound that we write *h*, also a large number of special articulations in the mouth chamber, like *p* and *s*. On the other hand, the glottal cords may be brought tight together, without vibrating. When this happens, the current of breath is checked for the time being. The slight choke or "arrested cough" that is thus made audible is not recognized in English as a definite sound but occurs nevertheless not infrequently. [[14]] This momentary check, technically known as a "glottal stop," is an integral element of speech in many languages, as Danish, Lettish, certain Chinese dialects, and nearly all American Indian languages. Between the two extremes of voicelessness, that of completely open breath and that of checked breath, lies the position of true voice. In this position the cords are close together, but not so tightly as to prevent the air from streaming through; the cords are set vibrating and a musical tone of varying pitch results. A tone so produced is known as a "voiced sound." It may have an indefinite number of qualities according to the precise position of the upper organs of speech. Our vowels, nasals (such as *m* and *n*), and such sounds as *b*, *z*, and *l* are all voiced sounds. The most convenient test of a voiced sound is the possibility of pronouncing it on any given pitch, in other words, of singing on it. [[15]] The voiced sounds are the most clearly audible elements of speech. As such they are the carriers of practically all significant differences in stress, pitch, and syllabification. The voiceless sounds are articulated noises that break up the stream of voice with fleeting moments of silence. Acoustically intermediate between the freely unvoiced and the voiced sounds are a number of other characteristic types of voicing, such as murmuring and whisper. [[16]] These and still other types of voice are relatively unimportant in English and most other European languages, but there are languages in which they rise to some prominence in the normal flow of speech.

The nose is not an active organ of speech, but it is highly important as a resonance chamber. It may be disconnected from the mouth, which is the other great resonance chamber, by the lifting of the movable part of the soft palate so as to shut off the passage of the breath into the nasal cavity; or, if the soft palate is allowed to hang down freely and unobstructively, so that the breath passes into both the nose and the mouth, these make a combined resonance chamber. Such sounds as *b* and *a* (as in *father*) are voiced "oral" sounds, that is, the voiced breath does not receive a nasal resonance. As soon as the soft palate is lowered, however, and the nose added as a participating resonance chamber, the sounds *b* and *a* take on a peculiar "nasal" quality and become, respectively, *m* and the nasalized vowel written *an* in French (e.g., *sang, tant*). The only English sounds [[17]] that normally receive a nasal resonance are *m, n,* and the *ng* sound of *sing*. Practically all sounds, however, may be nasalized, not only the vowels—nasalized vowels are common in all parts of the world—but such sounds as *l* or *z*. Voiceless nasals are perfectly possible. They occur, for instance, in Welsh and in quite a number of American Indian languages.

The organs that make up the oral resonance chamber may articulate in two ways. The breath, voiced or unvoiced, nasalized or unnasalized, may be allowed to pass through the mouth without being checked or impeded at any point; or it may be either momentarily checked or allowed to stream through a greatly narrowed passage with resulting air friction. There are also transitions between the two latter types of articulation. The unimpeded breath takes on a particular color or quality in accordance with the varying shape of the oral resonance chamber. This shape is chiefly determined by the position of the movable parts—the tongue and the lips. As the tongue is raised or lowered, retracted or brought forward, held tense or lax, and as the lips are pursed ("rounded") in varying degree or allowed to keep their position of rest, a large number of distinct qualities result. These oral qualities are the vowels. In theory their number is infinite, in practice the ear can differentiate only a limited, yet a surprisingly large, number of resonance positions. Vowels, whether nasalized or not, are normally voiced sounds; in not a few languages, however, "voiceless vowels" [[18]] also occur.

The remaining oral sounds are generally grouped together as "consonants." In them the stream of breath is interfered with in some way, so that a lesser resonance results, and a sharper, more incisive quality of tone. There are four main types of articulation generally recognized within the consonantal group of sounds. The breath may be completely stopped for a moment at some definite point in the oral cavity. Sounds so produced, like *t* or *d* or *p,* are known as "stops" or "explosives." [[19]] Or the breath may be continuously obstructed through a narrow passage, not entirely checked. Examples of such "spirants" or "fricatives," as they are called, are *s* and *z* and *y*. The third class of consonants, the "laterals," are semi-stopped. There is a true stoppage at the central point of articulation, but the breath is allowed to escape through the two side passages or through one of them. Our English *d*, for instance, may be readily transformed into *l*, which has the voicing and the position of *d*, merely by depressing the sides of the tongue on either side of the point of contact sufficiently to allow the breath to come through. Laterals are possible in many distinct positions. They may be unvoiced (the Welsh *ll* is an example) as well as voiced. Finally, the stoppage of the breath may be rapidly intermittent; in other words, the active organ of contact—generally the point of the tongue, less often the uvula [20]—may be made to vibrate against or near the point of contact. These sounds are the "trills" or "rolled consonants," of which the normal English *r* is a none too typical example. They are well developed in many languages, however, generally in voiced form, sometimes, as in Welsh and Paiute, in unvoiced form as well.

The oral manner of articulation is naturally not sufficient to define a consonant. The place of articulation must also be considered. Contacts may be formed at a large number of points, from the root of the tongue to the lips. It is not necessary here to go at length into this somewhat complicated matter. The contact is either between the root of the tongue and the throat, [21] some part of the tongue and a point on the palate (as in *k* or *ch* or *l*), some part of the tongue and the teeth (as in the English *th* of *thick* and *then*), the teeth and one of the lips (practically always the upper teeth and lower lip, as in *f*), or the two lips (as in *p* or English *w*). The tongue articulations are the most complicated of all, as the mobility of the tongue allows various points on its surface, say the tip, to articulate against a number of opposed points of contact. Hence arise many positions of articulation that we are not familiar with, such as the typical "dental" position of Russian or Italian *t* and *d*; or the "cerebral" position of Sanskrit and other languages of India, in which the tip of the tongue articulates against the hard palate. As there is no break at any point between the rims of the teeth back to the uvula nor from the tip of the tongue back to its root, it is evident that all the articulations that involve the tongue form a continuous organic (and acoustic) series. The positions grade into each other, but each language selects a limited number of clearly defined positions as characteristic of its consonantal system, ignoring transitional or extreme positions. Frequently a language allows a certain latitude in the fixing of the required position. This is true, for instance, of the English *k* sound, which is articulated much further to the front in a word like *kin* than in *cool*. We ignore this difference, psychologically, as a non-essential, mechanical one. Another language might well recognize the difference, or only a slightly greater one, as significant, as paralleling the distinction in position between the *k* of *kin* and the *t* of *tin*.

The organic classification of speech sounds is a simple matter after what we have learned of their production. Any such sound may be put into its proper place by the appropriate answer to four main questions:—What is the position of the glottal cords during its articulation? Does the breath pass into the mouth alone or is it also allowed to stream into the nose? Does the breath pass freely through the mouth or is it impeded at some point and, if so, in what manner? What are the precise points of articulation in the mouth?[[22]] This fourfold classification of sounds, worked out in all its detailed ramifications,[[23]] is sufficient to account for all, or practically all, the sounds of language.[[24]]

The phonetic habits of a given language are not exhaustively defined by stating that it makes use of such and such particular sounds out of the all but endless gamut that we have briefly surveyed. There remains the important question of the dynamics of these phonetic elements. Two languages may, theoretically, be built up of precisely the same series of consonants and vowels and yet produce utterly different acoustic effects. One of them may not recognize striking variations in the lengths or "quantities" of the phonetic elements, the other may note such variations most punctiliously (in probably the majority of languages long and short vowels are distinguished; in many, as in Italian or Swedish or Ojibwa, long consonants are recognized as distinct from short ones). Or the one, say English, may be very sensitive to relative stresses, while in the other, say French, stress is a very minor consideration. Or, again, the pitch differences which are inseparable from the actual practice of language may not affect the word as such, but, as in English, may be a more or less random or, at best, but a rhetorical phenomenon, while in other languages, as in Swedish, Lithuanian, Chinese, Siamese, and the majority of African languages, they may be more finely graduated and felt as integral characteristics of the words themselves. Varying methods of syllabifying are also responsible for noteworthy acoustic differences. Most important of all, perhaps, are the very different possibilities of combining the phonetic elements. Each language has its peculiarities. The *ts* combination, for instance, is found in both English and German, but in English it can only occur at the end of a word (as in *hats*), while it occurs freely in German as the psychological equivalent of a single sound (as in *Zeit, Katze*). Some languages allow of great heapings of consonants or of vocalic groups (diphthongs), in others no two consonants or no two vowels may ever come together. Frequently a sound occurs only in a special position or under special phonetic circumstances. In English, for instance, the *z*-sound of *azure* cannot occur initially, while the peculiar quality of the *t* of *sting* is dependent on its being preceded by the *s*. These dynamic factors, in their totality, are as important for the proper understanding of the phonetic genius of a language as the sound system itself, often far more so.

We have already seen, in an incidental way, that phonetic elements or such dynamic features as quantity and stress have varying psychological "values." The English *ts* of *fiats* is merely a *t* followed by a functionally independent *s*, the *ts* of the German word *Zeit* has an integral value equivalent, say, to the *t* of the English word *tide*. Again, the *t* of *time* is indeed noticeably distinct from that of *sting*, but the difference, to the consciousness of an English-speaking person, is quite irrelevant. It has no "value." If we compare the *t*-sounds of Haida, the Indian language spoken in the Queen Charlotte Islands, we find that precisely the same difference of articulation has a real value. In such a word as *sting* "two," the *t* is pronounced precisely as in English, but in *sta* "from" the *t* is clearly "aspirated," like that of *time*. In other words, an objective difference that is irrelevant in English is of functional value in Haida; from its own psychological standpoint the *t* of *sting* is as different from that of *sta* as, from our standpoint, is the *t* of *time* from the *d* of *divine*. Further investigation would yield the interesting result that the Haida ear finds the difference between the English *t* of *sting* and the *d* of *divine* as irrelevant as the naïve English ear finds that of the *t*-sounds of *sting* and *time*. The objective comparison of sounds in two or more languages is, then, of no psychological or historical significance unless these sounds are first "weighted," unless their phonetic "values" are determined. These values, in turn, flow from the general behavior and functioning of the sounds in actual speech.

These considerations as to phonetic value lead to an important conception. Back of the purely objective system of sounds that is peculiar to a language and which can be arrived at only by a painstaking phonetic analysis, there is a more restricted "inner" or "ideal" system which, while perhaps equally unconscious as a system to the naïve speaker, can far more readily than the other be brought to his consciousness as a finished pattern, a psychological mechanism. The inner sound-system, overlaid though it may be by the mechanical or the irrelevant, is a real and an immensely important principle in the life of a language. It may persist as a pattern, involving number, relation, and functioning of phonetic elements, long after its phonetic content is changed. Two historically related languages or dialects may not have a sound in common, but their ideal sound-systems may be identical patterns. I would not for a moment wish to imply that this pattern may not change. It may shrink or expand or change its functional complexion, but its rate of change is infinitely less rapid than that of the sounds as such. Every language, then, is characterized as much by its ideal system of sounds and by the underlying phonetic pattern (system, one might term it, of symbolic atoms) as by a definite grammatical structure. Both the phonetic and conceptual structures show the instinctive feeling of language for form. [25]

Form in Language: Grammatical Processes

The question of form in language presents itself under two aspects. We may either consider the formal methods employed by a language, its "grammatical processes," or we may ascertain the distribution of concepts with reference to formal expression. What are the formal patterns of the language? And what types of concepts make up the content of these formal patterns? The two points of view are quite distinct. The English word *unthinkingly* is, broadly speaking, formally parallel to the word *reformers*, each being built up on a radical element which may occur as an independent verb (*think, form*), this radical element being preceded by an element (*un-, re-*) that conveys a definite and fairly concrete significance but that cannot be used independently, and followed by two elements (*-ing, -ly; -er, -s*) that limit the application of the radical concept in a relational sense. This formal pattern—(b) + A + (c) + (d)[26]—is a characteristic feature of the language. A countless number of functions may be expressed by it; in other words, all the possible ideas conveyed by such prefixed and suffixed elements, while tending to fall into minor groups, do not necessarily form natural, functional systems. There is no logical reason, for instance, why the numeral function of *-s* should be formally expressed in a manner that is analogous to the expression of the idea conveyed by *-ly*. It is perfectly conceivable that in another language the concept of manner (*-ly*) may be treated according to an entirely different pattern from that of plurality. The former might have to be expressed by an independent word (say, *thus unthinking*), the latter by a prefixed element (say, *plural*[27]*-reform-er*). There are, of course, an unlimited number of other possibilities. Even within the confines of English alone the relative independence of form and function can be made obvious. Thus, the negative idea conveyed by *un-* can be just as adequately expressed by a suffixed element (*-less*) in such a word as *thoughtlessly*. Such a twofold formal expression of the negative function would be inconceivable in certain languages, say Eskimo, where a suffixed element would alone be possible. Again, the plural notion conveyed by the *-s* of *reformers* is just as definitely expressed in the word *geese*, where an utterly distinct method is employed. Furthermore, the principle of vocalic change (*goose—geese*) is by no means confined to the expression of the idea of plurality; it may also function as an indicator of difference of time (e.g., *sing—sang, throw—threw*). But the expression in English of past time is not by any means always bound up with a change of vowel. In the great majority of cases the same idea is expressed by means of a distinct suffix (*die-d, work-ed*). Functionally, *died* and *sang* are analogous; so are *reformers* and *geese*. Formally, we must arrange these words quite otherwise. Both *die-d* and *re-form-er-s* employ the method of suffixing grammatical elements; both *sang* and *geese* have grammatical form by virtue of the fact that their vowels differ from the vowels of other words with which they are closely related in form and meaning (*goose*; *sing, sung*).

Every language possesses one or more formal methods or indicating the relation of a secondary concept to the main concept of the radical element. Some of these grammatical processes, like suffixing, are exceedingly wide-spread; others, like vocalic change, are less common but far from rare; still others, like accent and consonantal change, are somewhat exceptional as functional processes. Not all languages are as irregular as English in the assignment of functions to its stock of grammatical processes. As a rule, such basic concepts as those of plurality and time are rendered by means of one or other method alone, but the rule has so many exceptions that we cannot safely lay it down as a principle. Wherever we go we are impressed by the fact that pattern is one thing, the utilization of pattern quite another. A few further examples of the multiple expression of identical functions in other languages than English may help to make still more vivid this idea of the relative independence of form and function.

In Hebrew, as in other Semitic languages, the verbal idea as such is expressed by three, less often by two or four, characteristic consonants. Thus, the group *sh-m-r* expresses the idea of "guarding," the group *g-n-b* that of "stealing," *n-t-n* that of "giving." Naturally these consonantal sequences are merely abstracted from the actual forms. The consonants are held together in different forms by characteristic vowels that vary according to the idea that it is desired to express. Prefixed and suffixed elements are also frequently used. The method of internal vocalic change is exemplified in *shamar* "he has guarded," *shomer* "guarding," *shamur* "being guarded," *shmor* "(to) guard." Analogously, *ganab* "he has stolen," *goneb* "stealing," *ganub* "being stolen," *gnob* "(to) steal." But not all infinitives are formed according to the type of *shmor* and *gnob* or of other types of internal vowel change. Certain verbs suffix a *t*-element for the infinitive, e.g., *ten-eth* "to give," *heyo-th* "to be." Again, the pronominal ideas may be expressed by independent words (e.g., *anoki* "I"), by prefixed elements (e.g., *e-shmor* "I shall guard"), or by suffixed elements (e.g., *shamar-ti* "I have guarded"). In Nass, an Indian language of British Columbia, plurals are formed by four distinct methods. Most nouns (and verbs) are reduplicated in the plural, that is, part of the radical element is repeated, e.g., *gyat* "person," *gyigyat* "people." A second method is the use of certain characteristic prefixes, e.g., *an'on* "hand," *ka-an'on* "hands"; *wai* "one paddles," *lu-wai* "several paddle." Still other plurals are formed by means of internal vowel change, e.g., *gwula* "cloak," *gwila* "cloaks." Finally, a fourth class of plurals is constituted by such nouns as suffix a grammatical element, e.g., *waky* "brother," *wakykw* "brothers."

From such groups of examples as these—and they might be multiplied *ad nauseam*—we cannot but conclude that linguistic form may and should be studied as types of patterning, apart from the associated functions. We are the more justified in this procedure as all languages evince a curious instinct for the development of one or more particular grammatical processes at the expense of others, tending always to lose sight of any explicit functional value that the process may have had in the first instance, delighting, it would seem, in the sheer play of its means of expression. It does not matter that in such a case as the English *goose—geese, foul—defile, sing—sang—sung* we can prove that we are dealing with historically distinct processes, that the vocalic alternation of *sing* and *sang*, for instance, is centuries older as a specific type of grammatical process than the outwardly parallel one of *goose* and *geese*. It remains true that there is (or was) an inherent tendency in English, at the time such forms as *geese* came into being, for the utilization of vocalic change as a significant linguistic method. Failing the precedent set by such already existing types of vocalic alternation as *sing—sang—sung*, it is highly doubtful if the detailed conditions that brought about the evolution of forms like *teeth* and *geese* from *tooth* and *goose* would have been potent enough to allow the native linguistic feeling to win through to an acceptance of these new types of plural formation as psychologically possible. This feeling for form as such, freely expanding along predetermined lines and greatly inhibited in certain directions by the lack of controlling types of patterning, should be more clearly understood than it seems to be. A general survey of many diverse types of languages is needed to give us the proper perspective on this point. We saw in the preceding chapter that every language has an inner phonetic system of definite pattern. We now learn that it has also a definite feeling for patterning on the level of grammatical formation. Both of these submerged and powerfully controlling impulses to definite form operate as such, regardless of the need for expressing particular concepts or of giving consistent external shape to particular groups of concepts. It goes without saying that these impulses can find realization only in concrete functional expression. We must say something to be able to say it in a certain manner.

Let us now take up a little more systematically, however briefly, the various grammatical processes that linguistic research has established. They may be grouped into six main types: word order; composition; affixation, including the use of prefixes, suffixes, and infixes; internal modification of the radical or grammatical element, whether this affects a vowel or a consonant; reduplication; and accentual differences, whether dynamic (stress) or tonal (pitch). There are also special quantitative processes, like vocalic lengthening or shortening and consonantal doubling, but these may be looked upon as particular sub-types of the process of internal modification. Possibly still other formal types exist, but they are not likely to be of importance in a general survey. It is important to bear in mind that a linguistic phenomenon cannot be looked upon as illustrating a definite "process" unless it has an inherent functional value. The consonantal change in English, for instance, of *book-s* and *bag-s* (*s* in the former, *z* in the latter) is of no functional significance. It is a purely external, mechanical change induced by the presence of a preceding voiceless consonant, *k*, in the former case, of a voiced consonant, *g*, in the latter. This mechanical alternation is objectively the same as that between the noun *house* and the verb *to house*. In the latter case, however, it has an important grammatical function, that of transforming a noun into a verb. The two alternations belong, then, to entirely different psychological categories. Only the latter is a true illustration of consonantal modification as a grammatical process.

The simplest, at least the most economical, method of conveying some sort of grammatical notion is to juxtapose two or more words in a definite sequence without making any attempt by inherent modification of these words to establish a connection between them. Let us put down two simple English words at random, say *sing praise*. This conveys no finished thought in English, nor does it clearly establish a relation between the idea of singing and that of praising. Nevertheless, it is psychologically impossible to hear or see the two words juxtaposed without straining to give them some measure of coherent significance. The attempt is not likely to yield an entirely satisfactory result, but what is significant is that as soon as two or more radical concepts are put before the human mind in immediate sequence it strives to bind them together with connecting values of some sort. In the case of *sing praise* different individuals are likely to arrive at different provisional results. Some of the latent possibilities of the juxtaposition, expressed in currently satisfying form, are: *sing praise (to him)!* or *singing praise, praise expressed in a song* or *to sing and praise* or *one who sings a song of praise* (compare such English compounds as *killjoy*, i.e., *one who kills joy*) or *he sings a song of praise (to him)*. The theoretical possibilities in the way of rounding out these two concepts into a significant group of concepts or even into a finished thought are indefinitely numerous. None of them will quite work in English, but there are numerous languages where one or other of these amplifying processes is habitual. It depends entirely on the genius of the particular language what function is inherently involved in a given sequence of words.

Some languages, like Latin, express practically all relations by means of modifications within the body of the word itself. In these, sequence is apt to be a rhetorical rather than a strictly grammatical principle. Whether I say in Latin *hominem femina videt* or *femina hominem videt* or *hominem videt femina* or *videt femina hominem* makes little or no difference beyond, possibly, a rhetorical or stylistic one. *The woman sees the man* is the identical significance of each of these sentences. In Chinook, an Indian language of the Columbia River, one can be equally free, for the relation between the verb and the two nouns is as inherently fixed as in Latin. The difference between the two languages is that, while Latin allows the nouns to establish their relation to each other and to the verb, Chinook lays the formal burden entirely on the verb, the full content of which is more or less adequately rendered by *she-him-sees*. Eliminate the Latin case suffixes (*-a* and *-em*) and the Chinook pronominal prefixes (*she-him-*) and we cannot afford to be so indifferent to our word order. We need to husband our resources. In other words, word order takes on a real functional value. Latin and Chinook are at one extreme. Such languages as Chinese, Siamese, and Annamite, in which each and every word, if it is to function properly, falls into its assigned place, are at the other extreme. But the majority of languages fall between these two extremes. In English, for instance, it may make little grammatical difference whether I say *yesterday the man saw the dog* or *the man saw the dog yesterday*, but it is not a matter of indifference whether I say *yesterday the man saw the dog* or *yesterday the dog saw the man* or whether I say *he is here* or *is he here?* In the one case, of the latter group of examples, the vital distinction of subject and object depends entirely on the placing of certain words of the sentence, in the latter a slight difference of sequence makes all the difference between statement and question. It goes without saying that in these cases the English principle of word order is as potent a means of expression as is the Latin use of case suffixes or of an interrogative particle. There is here no question of functional poverty, but of formal economy.

We have already seen something of the process of composition, the uniting into a single word of two or more radical elements. Psychologically this process is closely allied to that of word order in so far as the relation between the elements is implied, not explicitly stated. It differs from the mere juxtaposition of words in the sentence in that the compounded elements are felt as constituting but parts of a single word-organism. Such languages as Chinese and English, in which the principle of rigid sequence is well developed, tend not infrequently also to the development of compound words. It is but a step from such a Chinese word sequence as *jin tak* "man virtue," i.e., "the virtue of men," to such more conventionalized and psychologically unified juxtapositions as *t'ien tsz* "heaven son," i.e., "emperor," or *shui fu* "water man," i.e., "water carrier." In the latter case we may as well frankly write *shui-fu* as a single word, the meaning of the compound as a whole being as divergent from the precise etymological values of its component elements as is that of our English word *typewriter* from the merely combined values of *type* and *writer*. In English the unity of the word *typewriter* is further safeguarded by a predominant accent on the first syllable and by the possibility of adding such a suffixed element as the plural *-s* to the whole word. Chinese also unifies its compounds by means of stress. However, then, in its ultimate origins the process of composition may go back to typical sequences of words in the sentence, it is now, for the most part, a specialized method of expressing relations. French has as rigid a word order as English but does not possess anything like its power of compounding words into more complex units. On the other hand, classical Greek, in spite of its relative freedom in the placing of words, has a very considerable bent for the formation of compound terms.

It is curious to observe how greatly languages differ in their ability to make use of the process of composition. One would have thought on general principles that so simple a device as gives us our *typewriter* and *blackbird* and hosts of other words would be an all but universal grammatical process. Such is not the case. There are a great many languages, like Eskimo and Nootka and, aside from paltry exceptions, the Semitic languages, that cannot compound radical elements. What is even stranger is the fact that many of these languages are not in the least averse to complex word-formations, but may on the contrary effect a synthesis that far surpasses the utmost that Greek and Sanskrit are capable of. Such a Nootka word, for instance, as "when, as they say, he had been absent for four days" might be expected to embody at least three radical elements corresponding to the concepts of "absent," "four," and "day." As a matter of fact the Nootka word is utterly incapable of composition in our sense. It is invariably built up out of a single radical element and a greater or less number of suffixed elements, some of which may have as concrete a significance as the radical element itself. In, the particular case we have cited the radical element conveys the idea of "four," the notions of "day" and "absent" being expressed by suffixes that are as inseparable from the radical nucleus of the word as is an English element like *-er* from the *sing* or *hunt* of such words as *singer* and *hunter*. The tendency to word synthesis is, then, by no means the same thing as the tendency to compounding radical elements, though the latter is not infrequently a ready means for the synthetic tendency to work with.

There is a bewildering variety of types of composition. These types vary according to function, the nature of the compounded elements, and order. In a great many languages composition is confined to what we may call the delimiting function, that is, of the two or more compounded elements one is given a more precisely qualified significance by the others, which contribute nothing to the formal build of the sentence. In English, for instance, such compounded elements as *red* in *redcoat* or *over* in *overlook* merely modify the significance of the dominant *coat* or *look* without in any way sharing, as such, in the predication that is expressed by the sentence.

Some languages, however, such as Iroquois and Nahuatl,[28] employ the method of composition for much heavier work than this. In Iroquois, for instance, the composition of a noun, in its radical form, with a following verb is a typical method of expressing case relations, particularly of the subject or object. *I-meat-eat* for instance, is the regular Iroquois method of expressing the sentence *I am eating meat*. In other languages similar forms may express local or instrumental or still other relations. Such English forms as *killjoy* and *marplot* also illustrate the compounding of a verb and a noun, but the resulting word has a strictly nominal, not a verbal, function. We cannot say *he marplots*. Some languages allow the composition of all or nearly all types of elements. Paiute, for instance, may compound noun with noun, adjective with noun, verb with noun to make a noun, noun with verb to make a verb, adverb with verb, verb with verb. Yana, an Indian language of California, can freely compound noun with noun and verb with noun, but not verb with verb. On the other hand, Iroquois can compound only noun with verb, never noun and noun as in English or verb and verb as in so many other languages. Finally, each language has its characteristic types of order of composition. In English the qualifying element regularly precedes; in certain other languages it follows. Sometimes both types are used in the same language, as in Yana, where "beef" is "bitter-venison" but "deer-liver" is expressed by "liver-deer." The compounded object of a verb precedes the verbal element in Paiute, Nahuatl, and Iroquois, follows it in Yana, Tsimshian,[29] and the Algonkin languages.

Of all grammatical processes affixing is incomparably the most frequently employed. There are languages, like Chinese and Siamese, that make no grammatical use of elements that do not at the same time possess an independent value as radical elements, but such languages are uncommon. Of the three types of affixing—the use of prefixes, suffixes, and infixes—suffixing is much the commonest. Indeed, it is a fair guess that suffixes do more of the formative work of language than all other methods combined. It is worth noting that there are not a few affixing languages that make absolutely no use of prefixed elements but possess a complex apparatus of suffixes. Such are Turkish, Hottentot, Eskimo, Nootka, and Yana. Some of these, like the three last mentioned, have hundreds of suffixed elements, many of them of a concreteness of significance that would demand expression in the vast majority of languages by means of radical elements. The reverse case, the use of prefixed elements to the complete exclusion of suffixes, is far less common. A good example is Khmer (or Cambodgian), spoken in French Cochin-China, though even here there are obscure traces of old suffixes that have ceased to function as such and are now felt to form part of the radical element.

A considerable majority of known languages are prefixing and suffixing at one and the same time, but the relative importance of the two groups of affixed elements naturally varies enormously. In some languages, such as Latin and Russian, the suffixes alone relate the word to the rest of the sentence, the prefixes being confined to the expression of such ideas as delimit the concrete significance of the radical element without influencing its bearing in the proposition. A Latin form like *remittebantur* "they were being sent back" may serve as an illustration of this type of distribution of elements. The prefixed element *re-* "back" merely qualifies to a certain extent the inherent significance of the radical element *mitt-* "send," while the suffixes *-eba-*, *-nt-*, and *-ur* convey the less concrete, more strictly formal, notions of time, person, plurality, and passivity.

On the other hand, there are languages, like the Bantu group of Africa or the Athabaskan languages [30] of North America, in which the grammatically significant elements precede, those that follow the radical element forming a relatively dispensable class. The Hupa word *te-s-e-ya-te* "I will go," for example, consists of a radical element *-ya-* "to go," three essential prefixes and a formally subsidiary suffix. The element *te-* indicates that the act takes place here and there in space or continuously over space; practically, it has no clear-cut significance apart from such verb stems as it is customary to connect it with. The second prefixed element, *-s-*, is even less easy to define. All we can say is that it is used in verb forms of "definite" time and that it marks action as in progress rather than as beginning or coming to an end. The third prefix, *-e-*, is a pronominal element, "I," which can be used only in "definite" tenses. It is highly important to understand that the use of *-e-* is conditional on that of *-s-* or of certain alternative prefixes and that *te-* also is in practice linked with *-s-*. The group *te-s-e-ya* is a firmly knit grammatical unit. The suffix *-te*, which indicates the future, is no more necessary to its formal balance than is the prefixed *re-* of the Latin word; it is not an element that is capable of standing alone but its function is materially delimiting rather than strictly formal. [31]

It is not always, however, that we can clearly set off the suffixes of a language as a group against its prefixes. In probably the majority of languages that use both types of affixes each group has both delimiting and formal or relational functions. The most that we can say is that a language tends to express similar functions in either the one or the other manner. If a certain verb expresses a certain tense by suffixing, the probability is strong that it expresses its other tenses in an analogous fashion and that, indeed, all verbs have suffixed tense elements. Similarly, we normally expect to find the pronominal elements, so far as they are included in the verb at all, either consistently prefixed or suffixed. But these rules are far from absolute. We have already seen that Hebrew prefixes its pronominal elements in certain cases, suffixes them in others. In Chimariko, an Indian language of California, the position of the pronominal affixes depends on the verb; they are prefixed for certain verbs, suffixed for others.

It will not be necessary to give many further examples of prefixing and suffixing. One of each category will suffice to illustrate their formative possibilities. The idea expressed in English by the sentence *I came to give it to her* is rendered in Chinook by *i-n-i-a-l-u-d-am*. This word—and it is a thoroughly unified word with a clear-cut accent on the first *a*—consists of a radical element, *-d-* "to give," six functionally distinct, if phonetically frail, prefixed elements, and a suffix. Of the prefixes, *i-* indicates recently past time; *n-*, the pronominal subject "I"; *-i-*, the pronominal object "it"; *-a-*, the second pronominal object "her"; *-l-*, a prepositional element indicating that the preceding pronominal prefix is to be understood as an indirect object (*-her-to-*, i.e., "to her"); and *-u-*, an element that it is not easy to define satisfactorily but which, on the whole, indicates movement away from the speaker. The suffixed *-am* modifies the verbal content in a local sense; it adds to the notion conveyed by the radical element that of "arriving" or "going (or coming) for that particular purpose." It is obvious that in Chinook, as in Hupa, the greater part of the grammatical machinery resides in the prefixes rather than in the suffixes.

A reverse case, one in which the grammatically significant elements cluster, as in Latin, at the end of the word is yielded by Fox, one of the better known Algonkin languages of the Mississippi Valley. We may take the form *eh-kiwi-n-a-m-oht-ati-wa-ch(i)* "then they together kept (him) in flight from them." The radical element here is *kiwi-*, a verb stem indicating the general notion of "indefinite movement round about, here and there."

The prefixed element *eh-* is hardly more than an adverbial particle indicating temporal subordination; it may be conveniently rendered as "then." Of the seven suffixes included in this highly-wrought word, *-n-* seems to be merely a phonetic element serving to connect the verb stem with the following *-a-*; [34] *-a-* is a "secondary stem" [35] denoting the idea of "flight, to flee"; *-m-* denotes causality with reference to an animate object; [36] *-o(ht)-* indicates activity done for the subject (the so-called "middle" or "medio-passive" voice of Greek); *-(a)ti-* is a reciprocal element, "one another"; *-wa-ch(i)* is the third person animate plural (*-wa-*, plural; *-chi*, more properly personal) of so-called "conjunctive" forms. The word may be translated more literally (and yet only approximately as to grammatical feeling) as "then they (animate) caused some animate being to wander about in flight from one another of themselves." Eskimo, Nootka, Yana, and other languages have similarly complex arrays of suffixed elements, though the functions performed by them and their principles of combination differ widely.

We have reserved the very curious type of affixation known as "infixing" for separate illustration. It is utterly unknown in English, unless we consider the *-n-* of *stand* (contrast *stood*) as an infixed element. The earlier Indo-European languages, such as Latin, Greek and Sanskrit, made a fairly considerable use of infixed nasals to differentiate the present tense of a certain class of verbs from other forms (contrast Latin *vinc-o* "I conquer" with *vic-i* "I conquered"; Greek *lamb-an-o* "I take" with *e-lab-on* "I took"). There are, however, more striking examples of the process, examples in which it has assumed a more clearly defined function than in these Latin and Greek cases. It is particularly prevalent in many languages of southeastern Asia and of the Malay archipelago. Good examples from Khmer (Cambodgian) are *tmeu* "one who walks" and *daneu* "walking" (verbal noun), both derived from *deu* "to walk." Further examples may be quoted from Bontoc Igorot, a Filipino language. Thus, an infixed *-in-* conveys the idea of the product of an accomplished action, e.g., *kayu* "wood," *kinayu* "gathered wood." Infixes are also freely used in the Bontoc Igorot verb. Thus, an infixed *-um-* is characteristic of many intransitive verbs with personal pronominal suffixes, e.g., *sad-* "to wait," *sumid-ak* "I wait"; *kineg* "silent," *kuminek-ak* "I am silent." In other verbs it indicates futurity, e.g., *tengao-* "to celebrate a holiday," *tumengao-ak* "I shall have a holiday." The past tense is frequently indicated by an infixed *-in-*; if there is already an infixed *-um-*, the two elements combine to *-in-m-*, e.g., *kinminek-ak* "I am silent." Obviously the infixing process has in this (and related) languages the same vitality that is possessed by the commoner prefixes and suffixes of other languages. The process is also found in a number of aboriginal American languages. The Yana plural is sometimes formed by an infixed element, e.g., *k'uruwi* "medicine-men," *k'uwi* "medicine-man"; in Chinook an infixed *-l-* is used in certain verbs to indicate repeated activity, e.g., *ksik'ludelk* "she keeps looking at him," *iksik'lutk* "she looked at him" (radical element *-tk*). A peculiarly interesting type of infixation is found in the Siouan languages, in which certain verbs insert the pronominal elements into the very body of the radical element, e.g., Sioux *cheti* "to build a fire," *chewati* "I build a fire"; *shuta* "to miss," *shuunta-pi* "we miss."

A subsidiary but by no means unimportant grammatical process is that of internal vocalic or consonantal change. In some languages, as in English (*sing, sang, sung, song*; *goose, geese*), the former of these has become one of the major methods of indicating fundamental changes of grammatical function. At any rate, the process is alive enough to lead our children into untrodden ways. We all know of the growing youngster who speaks of having *brung* something, on the analogy of such forms as *sung* and *flung*. In Hebrew, as we have seen, vocalic change is of even greater significance than in English. What is true of Hebrew is of course true of all other Semitic languages. A few examples of so-called "broken" plurals from Arabic [37] will supplement the Hebrew verb forms that I have given in another connection. The noun *balad* "place" has the plural form *bilad*; [38] *gild* "hide" forms the plural *gulud*; *ragil* "man," the plural *rigal*; *shibbak* "window," the plural *shababik*. Very similar phenomena are illustrated by the Hamitic languages of Northern Africa, e.g., Shilh [39] *izbil* "hair," plural *izbel*; *a-slem* "fish," plural *i-slim-en*; *sn* "to know," *sen* "to be knowing"; *rmi* "to become tired," *rumni* "to be tired"; *ttss* [40] "to fall asleep," *ttoss* "to sleep." Strikingly similar to English and Greek alternations of the type *sing—sang* and *leip-o* "I leave," *leloip-a* "I have left," are such Somali [41] cases as *al* "I am," *il* "I was"; *i-dah-a* "I say," *i-di* "I said," *deh* "say!"

Vocalic change is of great significance also in a number of American Indian languages. In the Athabaskan group many verbs change the quality or quantity of the vowel of the radical element as it changes its tense or mode. The Navaho verb for "I put (grain) into a receptacle" is *bi-hi-sh-ja*, in which -*ja* is the radical element; the past tense, *bi-hi-ja'*, has a long *a*-vowel, followed by the "glottal stop" [[42]]; the future is *bi-h-de-sh-ji* with complete change of vowel. In other types of Navaho verbs the vocalic changes follow different lines, e.g., *yah-a-ni-ye* "you carry (a pack) into (a stable)"; past, *yah-i-ni-yin* (with long *i* in *-yin*; *-n* is here used to indicate nasalization); future, *yah-a-di-yehl* (with long *e*). In another Indian language, Yokuts [[43]], vocalic modifications affect both noun and verb forms. Thus, *buchong* "son" forms the plural *bochang-i* (contrast the objective *buchong-a*); *enash* "grandfather," the plural *inash-a*; the verb *engtyim* "to sleep" forms the continuative *ingetym-ad* "to be sleeping" and the past *ingetym-ash*.

Consonantal change as a functional process is probably far less common than vocalic modifications, but it is not exactly rare. There is an interesting group of cases in English, certain nouns and corresponding verbs differing solely in that the final consonant is voiceless or voiced. Examples are *wreath* (with *th* as in *think*), but *to wreathe* (with *th* as in *then*); *house*, but *to house* (with *s* pronounced like *z*). That we have a distinct feeling for the interchange as a means of distinguishing the noun from the verb is indicated by the extension of the principle by many Americans to such a noun as *rise* (e.g., *the rise of democracy*)—pronounced like *rice*—in contrast to the verb *to rise* (*s* like *z*).

In the Celtic languages the initial consonants undergo several types of change according to the grammatical relation that subsists between the word itself and the preceding word. Thus, in modern Irish, a word like *bo* "ox" may under the appropriate circumstances, take the forms *bho* (pronounce *wo*) or *mo* (e.g., *an bo* "the ox," as a subject, but *tir na mo* "land of the oxen," as a possessive plural). In the verb the principle has as one of its most striking consequences the "aspiration" of initial consonants in the past tense. If a verb begins with *t*, say, it changes the *t* to *th* (now pronounced *h*) in forms of the past; if it begins with *g*, the consonant changes, in analogous forms, to *gh* (pronounced like a voiced spirant [[44]] *g* or like *y*, according to the nature of the following vowel). In modern Irish the principle of consonantal change, which began in the oldest period of the language as a secondary consequence of certain phonetic conditions, has become one of the primary grammatical processes of the language.

Perhaps as remarkable as these Irish phenomena are the consonantal interchanges of Ful, an African language of the Soudan. Here we find that all nouns belonging to the personal class form the plural by changing their initial *g, j, d, b, k, ch*, and *p* to *y* (or *w*), *y, r, w, h, s* and *f* respectively; e.g., *jim-o* "companion," *yim-'be* "companions"; *pio-o* "beater," *fio-'be* "beaters." Curiously enough, nouns that belong to the class of things form their singular and plural in exactly reverse fashion, e.g., *yola-re* "grass-grown place," *jola-je* "grass-grown places"; *fitan-du* "soul," *pital-i* "souls." In Nootka, to refer to but one other language in which the process is found, the *t* or *tl* [45] of many verbal suffixes becomes *hl* in forms denoting repetition, e.g., *hita-'ato* "to fall out," *hita-'ahl* "to keep falling out"; *mat-achisht-utl* "to fly on to the water," *mat-achisht-ohl* "to keep flying on to the water." Further, the *hl* of certain elements changes to a peculiar *h*-sound in plural forms, e.g., *yak-ohl* "sore-faced," *yak-oh* "sore-faced (people)."

Nothing is more natural than the prevalence of reduplication, in other words, the repetition of all or part of the radical element. The process is generally employed, with self-evident symbolism, to indicate such concepts as distribution, plurality, repetition, customary activity, increase of size, added intensity, continuance. Even in English it is not unknown, though it is not generally accounted one of the typical formative devices of our language. Such words as *goody-goody* and *to pooh-pooh* have become accepted as part of our normal vocabulary, but the method of duplication may on occasion be used more freely than is indicated by such stereotyped examples. Such locutions as *a big big man* or *Let it cool till it's thick thick* are far more common, especially in the speech of women and children, than our linguistic text-books would lead one to suppose. In a class by themselves are the really enormous number of words, many of them sound-imitative or contemptuous in psychological tone, that consist of duplications with either change of the vowel or change of the initial consonant—words of the type *sing-song, riff-raff, wishy-washy, harum-skarum, roly-poly*. Words of this type are all but universal. Such examples as the Russian *Chudo-Yudo* (a dragon), the Chinese *ping-pang* "rattling of rain on the roof," [46] the Tibetan *kyang-kyong* "lazy," and the Manchu *porpon parpan* "blear-eyed" are curiously reminiscent, both in form and in psychology, of words nearer home. But it can hardly be said that the duplicative process is of a distinctively grammatical significance in English. We must turn to other languages for illustration. Such cases as Hottentot *go-go* "to look at carefully" (from *go* "to see"), Somali *fen-fen* "to gnaw at on all sides" (from *fen* "to gnaw at"), Chinook *iwi iwi* "to look about carefully, to examine" (from *iwi* "to appear"), or Tsimshian *am'am* "several (are) good" (from *am* "good") do not depart from the natural and fundamental range of significance of the process. A more abstract function is illustrated in Ewe,[47] in which both infinitives and verbal adjectives are formed from verbs by duplication; e.g., *yi* "to go," *yiyi* "to go, act of going"; *wo* "to do," *wowo*[48] "done"; *mawomawo* "not to do" (with both duplicated verb stem and duplicated negative particle). Causative duplications are characteristic of Hottentot, e.g., *gam-gam*[49] "to cause to tell" (from *gam* "to tell"). Or the process may be used to derive verbs from nouns, as in Hottentot *khoe-khoe* "to talk Hottentot" (from *khoe-b* "man, Hottentot"), or as in Kwakiutl *metmat* "to eat clams" (radical element *met-* "clam").

The most characteristic examples of reduplication are such as repeat only part of the radical element. It would be possible to demonstrate the existence of a vast number of formal types of such partial duplication, according to whether the process makes use of one or more of the radical consonants, preserves or weakens or alters the radical vowel, or affects the beginning, the middle, or the end of the radical element. The functions are even more exuberantly developed than with simple duplication, though the basic notion, at least in origin, is nearly always one of repetition or continuance. Examples illustrating this fundamental function can be quoted from all parts of the globe. Initially reduplicating are, for instance, Shilh *ggen* "to be sleeping" (from *gen* "to sleep"); Ful *pepeu-'do* "liar" (i.e., "one who always lies"), plural *fefeu-'be* (from *fewa* "to lie"); Bontoc Igorot *anak* "child," *ananak* "children"; *kamu-ek* "I hasten," *kakamu-ek* "I hasten more"; Tsimshian *gyad* "person," *gyigyad* "people"; Nass *gyibayuk* "to fly," *gyigyibayuk* "one who is flying." Psychologically comparable, but with the reduplication at the end, are Somali *ur* "body," plural *urar*; Hausa *suna* "name," plural *sunana-ki;* Washo[50] *gusu* "buffalo," *gususu* "buffaloes"; Takelma[51] *himi-d-* "to talk to," *himim-d-* "to be accustomed to talk to." Even more commonly than simple duplication, this partial duplication of the radical element has taken on in many languages functions that seem in no way related to the idea of increase. The best known examples are probably the initial reduplication of our older Indo-European languages, which helps to form the perfect tense of many verbs (e.g., Sanskrit *dadarsha* "I have seen," Greek *leloipa* "I have left," Latin *tetigi* "I have touched," Gothic *lelot* "I have let"). In Nootka reduplication of the radical element is often employed in association with certain suffixes; e.g., *hluch-*

"woman" forms *hluhluch-'ituhl* "to dream of a woman," *hluhluch-k'ok* "resembling a woman." Psychologically similar to the Greek and Latin examples are many Takelma cases of verbs that exhibit two forms of the stem, one employed in the present or past, the other in the future and in certain modes and verbal derivatives. The former has final reduplication, which is absent in the latter; e.g., *al-yebeb-i'n* "I show (or showed) to him," *al-yeb-in* "I shall show him."

We come now to the subtlest of all grammatical processes, variations in accent, whether of stress or pitch. The chief difficulty in isolating accent as a functional process is that it is so often combined with alternations in vocalic quantity or quality or complicated by the presence of affixed elements that its grammatical value appears as a secondary rather than as a primary feature. In Greek, for instance, it is characteristic of true verbal forms that they throw the accent back as far as the general accentual rules will permit, while nouns may be more freely accented. There is thus a striking accentual difference between a verbal form like *eluthemen* "we were released," accented on the second syllable of the word, and its participial derivative *lutheis* "released," accented on the last. The presence of the characteristic verbal elements *e-* and *-men* in the first case and of the nominal *-s* in the second tends to obscure the inherent value of the accentual alternation. This value comes out very neatly in such English doublets as *to refund* and *a refund, to extract* and *an extract, to come down* and *a come down, to lack luster* and *lack-luster eyes*, in which the difference between the verb and the noun is entirely a matter of changing stress. In the Athabaskan languages there are not infrequently significant alternations of accent, as in Navaho *ta-di-gis* "you wash yourself" (accented on the second syllable), *ta-di-gis* "he washes himself" (accented on the first). [52]

Pitch accent may be as functional as stress and is perhaps more often so. The mere fact, however, that pitch variations are phonetically essential to the language, as in Chinese (e.g., *feng* "wind" with a level tone, *feng* "to serve" with a falling tone) or as in classical Greek (e.g., *lab-on* "having taken" with a simple or high tone on the suffixed participial *-on*, *gunaik-on* "of women" with a compound or falling tone on the case suffix *-on*) does not necessarily constitute a functional, or perhaps we had better say grammatical, use of pitch. In such cases the pitch is merely inherent in the radical element or affix, as any vowel or consonant might be. It is different with such Chinese alternations as *chung* (level) "middle" and *chung* (falling) "to hit the middle"; *mai* (rising) "to buy" and *mai* (falling) "to sell"; *pei* (falling) "back" and *pei* (level) "to carry on the back." Examples of this type are not exactly common in Chinese and the language cannot be said to possess at present a definite feeling for tonal differences as symbolic of the distinction between noun and verb.

There are languages, however, in which such differences are of the most fundamental grammatical importance. They are particularly common in the Soudan. In Ewe, for instance, there are formed from *subo* "to serve" two reduplicated forms, an infinitive *subosubo* "to serve," with a low tone on the first two syllables and a high one on the last two, and an adjectival *subosubo* "serving," in which all the syllables have a high tone. Even more striking are cases furnished by Shilluk, one of the languages of the headwaters of the Nile. The plural of the noun often differs in tone from the singular, e.g., *yit* (high) "ear" but *yit* (low) "ears." In the pronoun three forms may be distinguished by tone alone; *e* "he" has a high tone and is subjective, *-e* "him" (e.g., *a chwol-e* "he called him") has a low tone and is objective, *-e* "his" (e.g., *wod-e* "his house") has a middle tone and is possessive. From the verbal element *gwed-* "to write" are formed *gwed-o* "(he) writes" with a low tone, the passive *gwet* "(it was) written" with a falling tone, the imperative *gwet* "write!" with a rising tone, and the verbal noun *gwet* "writing" with a middle tone. In aboriginal America also pitch accent is known to occur as a grammatical process. A good example of such a pitch language is Tlingit, spoken by the Indians of the southern coast of Alaska. In this language many verbs vary the tone of the radical element according to tense; *hun* "to sell," *sin* "to hide," *tin* "to see," and numerous other radical elements, if low-toned, refer to past time, if high-toned, to the future. Another type of function is illustrated by the Takelma forms *hel* "song," with falling pitch, but *hel* "sing!" with a rising inflection; parallel to these forms are *sel* (falling) "black paint," *sel* (rising) "paint it!" All in all it is clear that pitch accent, like stress and vocalic or consonantal modifications, is far less infrequently employed as a grammatical process than our own habits of speech would prepare us to believe probable.

Form in Language: Grammatical Concepts

We have seen that the single word expresses either a simple concept or a combination of concepts so interrelated as to form a psychological unity. We have, furthermore, briefly reviewed from a strictly formal standpoint the main processes that are used by all known languages to affect the fundamental concepts—those embodied in unanalyzable words or in the radical elements of words—by the modifying or formative influence of subsidiary concepts. In this chapter we shall look a little more closely into the nature of the world of concepts, in so far as that world is reflected and systematized in linguistic structure.

Let us begin with a simple sentence that involves various kinds of concepts—*the farmer kills the duckling*. A rough and ready analysis discloses here the presence of three distinct and fundamental concepts that are brought into connection with each other in a number of ways. These three concepts are "farmer" (the subject of discourse), "kill" (defining the nature of the activity which the sentence informs us about), and "duckling" (another subject [53] of discourse that takes an important though somewhat passive part in this activity). We can visualize the farmer and the duckling and we have also no difficulty in constructing an image of the killing. In other words, the elements *farmer*, *kill*, and *duckling* define concepts of a concrete order.

But a more careful linguistic analysis soon brings us to see that the two subjects of discourse, however simply we may visualize them, are not expressed quite as directly, as immediately, as we feel them. A "farmer" is in one sense a perfectly unified concept, in another he is "one who farms." The concept conveyed by the radical element (*farm-*) is not one of personality at all but of an industrial activity (*to farm*), itself based on the concept of a particular type of object (*a farm*). Similarly, the concept of *duckling* is at one remove from that which is expressed by the radical element of the word, *duck*. This element, which may occur as an independent word, refers to a whole class of animals, big and little, while *duckling* is limited in its application to the young of that class. The word *farmer* has an "agentive" suffix *-er* that performs the function of indicating the one that carries out a given activity, in this case that of farming. It transforms the verb *to farm* into an agentive noun precisely as it transforms the verbs *to sing, to paint, to teach* into the corresponding agentive nouns *singer, painter, teacher*. The element *-ling* is not so freely used, but its significance is obvious. It adds to the basic concept the notion of smallness (as also in *gosling, fledgeling*) or the somewhat related notion of "contemptible" (as in *weakling, princeling, hireling*). The agentive *-er* and the diminutive *-ling* both convey fairly concrete ideas (roughly those of "doer" and "little"), but the concreteness is not stressed. They do not so much define distinct concepts as mediate between concepts. The *-er* of *farmer* does not quite say "one who (farms)" it merely indicates that the sort of person we call a "farmer" is closely enough associated with activity on a farm to be conventionally thought of as always so occupied. He may, as a matter of fact, go to town and engage in any pursuit but farming, yet his linguistic label remains "farmer." Language here betrays a certain helplessness or, if one prefers, a stubborn tendency to look away from the immediately suggested function, trusting to the imagination and to usage to fill in the transitions of thought and the details of application that distinguish one concrete concept (*to farm*) from another "derived" one (*farmer*). It would be impossible for any language to express every concrete idea by an independent word or radical element. The concreteness of experience is infinite, the resources of the richest language are strictly limited. It must perforce throw countless concepts under the rubric of certain basic ones, using other concrete or semi-concrete ideas as functional mediators. The ideas expressed by these mediating elements—they may be independent words, affixes, or modifications of the radical element—may be called "derivational" or "qualifying." Some concrete concepts, such as *kill*, are expressed radically; others, such as *farmer* and *duckling*, are expressed derivatively. Corresponding to these two modes of expression we have two types of concepts and of linguistic elements, radical (*farm, kill, duck*) and derivational (*-er, -ling*). When a word (or unified group of words) contains a derivational element (or word) the concrete significance of the radical element (*farm-, duck-*) tends to fade from consciousness and to yield to a new concreteness (*farmer, duckling*) that is synthetic in expression rather than in thought. In our sentence the concepts of *farm* and *duck* are not really involved at all; they are merely latent, for formal reasons, in the linguistic expression.

Returning to this sentence, we feel that the analysis of *farmer* and *duckling* are practically irrelevant to an understanding of its content and entirely irrelevant to a feeling for the structure of the sentence as a whole. From the standpoint of the sentence the derivational elements *-er* and *-ling* are merely details in the local economy of two of its terms (*farmer*, *duckling*) that it accepts as units of expression. This indifference of the sentence as such to some part of the analysis of its words is shown by the fact that if we substitute such radical words as *man* and *chick* for *farmer* and *duckling*, we obtain a new material content, it is true, but not in the least a new structural mold. We can go further and substitute another activity for that of "killing," say "taking." The new sentence, *the man takes the chick*, is totally different from the first sentence in what it conveys, not in how it conveys it. We feel instinctively, without the slightest attempt at conscious analysis, that the two sentences fit precisely the same pattern, that they are really the same fundamental sentence, differing only in their material trappings. In other words, they express identical relational concepts in an identical manner. The manner is here threefold—the use of an inherently relational word (*the*) in analogous positions, the analogous sequence (subject; predicate, consisting of verb and object) of the concrete terms of the sentence, and the use of the suffixed element *-s* in the verb.

Change any of these features of the sentence and it becomes modified, slightly or seriously, in some purely relational, non-material regard. If *the* is omitted (*farmer kills duckling*, *man takes chick*), the sentence becomes impossible; it falls into no recognized formal pattern and the two subjects of discourse seem to hang incompletely in the void. We feel that there is no relation established between either of them and what is already in the minds of the speaker and his auditor. As soon as a *the* is put before the two nouns, we feel relieved. We know that the farmer and duckling which the sentence tells us about are the same farmer and duckling that we had been talking about or hearing about or thinking about some time before. If I meet a man who is not looking at and knows nothing about the farmer in question, I am likely to be stared at for my pains if I announce to him that "the farmer [what farmer?] the duckling [didn't know he had any, whoever he is]." If the fact nevertheless seems interesting enough to communicate, I should be compelled to speak of "*a farmer* up my way" and of "*a duckling* of his."

These little words, *the* and *a*, have the important function of establishing a definite or an indefinite reference.

If I omit the first *the* and also leave out the suffixed *-s*, I obtain an entirely new set of relations. *Farmer, kill the duckling* implies that I am now speaking to the farmer, not merely about him; further, that he is not actually killing the bird, but is being ordered by me to do so. The subjective relation of the first sentence has become a vocative one, one of address, and the activity is conceived in terms of command, not of statement. We conclude, therefore, that if the farmer is to be merely talked about, the little *the* must go back into its place and the *-s* must not be removed. The latter element clearly defines, or rather helps to define, statement as contrasted with command. I find, moreover, that if I wish to speak of several farmers, I cannot say *the farmers kills the duckling*, but must say *the farmers kill the duckling*. Evidently *-s* involves the notion of singularity in the subject. If the noun is singular, the verb must have a form to correspond; if the noun is plural, the verb has another, corresponding form. [[54]] Comparison with such forms as *I kill* and *you kill* shows, moreover, that the *-s* has exclusive reference to a person other than the speaker or the one spoken to. We conclude, therefore, that it connotes a personal relation as well as the notion of singularity. And comparison with a sentence like *the farmer killed the duckling* indicates that there is implied in this overburdened *-s* a distinct reference to present time. Statement as such and personal reference may well be looked upon as inherently relational concepts. Number is evidently felt by those who speak English as involving a necessary relation, otherwise there would be no reason to express the concept twice, in the noun and in the verb. Time also is clearly felt as a relational concept; if it were not, we should be allowed to say *the farmer killed-s* to correspond to *the farmer kill-s*. Of the four concepts inextricably interwoven in the *-s* suffix, all are felt as relational, two necessarily so. The distinction between a truly relational concept and one that is so felt and treated, though it need not be in the nature of things, will receive further attention in a moment.

Finally, I can radically disturb the relational cut of the sentence by changing the order of its elements. If the positions of *farmer* and *kills* are interchanged, the sentence reads *kills the farmer the duckling*, which is most naturally interpreted as an unusual but not unintelligible mode of asking the question, *does the farmer kill the duckling?* In this new sentence the act is not conceived as necessarily taking place at all. It may or it may not be happening, the implication being that the speaker wishes to know the truth of the matter and that the person spoken to is expected to give him the information. The interrogative sentence possesses an entirely different "modality" from the declarative one and implies a markedly different attitude of the speaker towards his companion. An even more striking change in personal relations is effected if we interchange *the farmer* and *the duckling*. *The duckling kills the farmer* involves precisely the same subjects of discourse and the same type of activity as our first sentence, but the rôles of these subjects of discourse are now reversed. The duckling has turned, like the proverbial worm, or, to put it in grammatical terminology, what was "subject" is now "object," what was object is now subject.

The following tabular statement analyzes the sentence from the point of view of the concepts expressed in it and of the grammatical processes employed for their expression.

I. CONCRETE CONCEPTS:
    1. First subject of discourse: *farmer*
    2. Second subject of discourse: *duckling*
    3. Activity: *kill*
    —— analyzable into:
  A. RADICAL CONCEPTS:
    1. Verb: *(to) farm*
    2. Noun: *duck*
    3. Verb: *kill*
  B. DERIVATIONAL CONCEPTS:
    1. Agentive: expressed by suffix *-er*
    2. Diminutive: expressed by suffix *-ling*

II. RELATIONAL CONCEPTS:

Reference:

    1. Definiteness of reference to first subject of discourse: expressed by first *the*, which has preposed position
    2. Definiteness of reference to second subject of discourse: expressed by second *the*, which has preposed position

Modality:
3. Declarative: expressed by sequence of "subject" plus verb; and implied by suffixed -s

Personal relations:
4. Subjectivity of *farmer*: expressed by position of *farmer* before kills; and by suffixed -s
5. Objectivity of *duckling*: expressed by position of *duckling* after *kills*

Number:
6. Singularity of first subject of discourse: expressed by lack of plural suffix in *farmer*; and by suffix -s in following verb
7. Singularity of second subject of discourse: expressed by lack of plural suffix in *duckling*

Time:
8. Present: expressed by lack of preterit suffix in verb; and by suffixed -s

In this short sentence of five words there are expressed, therefore, thirteen distinct concepts, of which three are radical and concrete, two derivational, and eight relational. Perhaps the most striking result of the analysis is a renewed realization of the curious lack of accord in our language between function and form. The method of suffixing is used both for derivational and for relational elements; independent words or radical elements express both concrete ideas (objects, activities, qualities) and relational ideas (articles like *the* and *a*; words defining case relations, like *of, to, for, with, by*; words defining local relations, like *in, on, at*); the same relational concept may be expressed more than once (thus, the singularity of *farmer* is both negatively expressed in the noun and positively in the verb); and one element may convey a group of interwoven concepts rather than one definite concept alone (thus the -s of *kills* embodies no less than four logically independent relations).

Our analysis may seem a bit labored, but only because we are so accustomed to our own well-worn grooves of expression that they have come to be felt as inevitable. Yet destructive analysis of the familiar is the only method of approach to an understanding of fundamentally different modes of expression. When one has learned to feel what is fortuitous or illogical or unbalanced in the structure of his own language, he is already well on the way towards a sympathetic grasp of the expression of the various classes of concepts in alien types of speech. Not everything that is "outlandish" is intrinsically illogical or far-fetched. It is often precisely the familiar that a wider perspective reveals as the curiously exceptional. From a purely logical standpoint it is obvious that there is no inherent reason why the concepts expressed in our sentence should have been singled out, treated, and grouped as they have been and not otherwise. The sentence is the outgrowth of historical and of unreasoning psychological forces rather than of a logical synthesis of elements that have been clearly grasped in their individuality. This is the case, to a greater or less degree, in all languages, though in the forms of many we find a more coherent, a more consistent, reflection than in our English forms of that unconscious analysis into individual concepts which is never entirely absent from speech, however it may be complicated with or overlaid by the more irrational factors.

A cursory examination of other languages, near and far, would soon show that some or all of the thirteen concepts that our sentence happens to embody may not only be expressed in different form but that they may be differently grouped among themselves; that some among them may be dispensed with; and that other concepts, not considered worth expressing in English idiom, may be treated as absolutely indispensable to the intelligible rendering of the proposition. First as to a different method of handling such concepts as we have found expressed in the English sentence. If we turn to German, we find that in the equivalent sentence (*Der Bauer tötet das Entelein*) the definiteness of reference expressed by the English *the* is unavoidably coupled with three other concepts—number (both *der* and *das* are explicitly singular), case (*der* is subjective; *das* is subjective or objective, by elimination therefore objective), and gender, a new concept of the relational order that is not in this case explicitly involved in English (*der* is masculine, *das* is neuter). Indeed, the chief burden of the expression of case, gender, and number is in the German sentence borne by the particles of reference rather than by the words that express the concrete concepts (*Bauer, Entelein*) to which these relational concepts ought logically to attach themselves. In the sphere of concrete concepts too it is worth noting that the German splits up the idea of "killing" into the basic concept of "dead" (*tot*) and the derivational one of "causing to do (or be) so and so" (by the method of vocalic change, *töt-*); the German *töt-et* (analytically *tot-*+vowel change+*-et*) "causes to be dead" is, approximately, the formal equivalent of our *dead-en-s*, though the idiomatic application of this latter word is different. [55]

Wandering still further afield, we may glance at the Yana method of expression. Literally translated, the equivalent Yana sentence would read something like "kill-s he farmer [56] he to duck-ling," in which "he" and "to" are rather awkward English renderings of a general third personal pronoun (*he, she, it,* or *they*) and an objective particle which indicates that the following noun is connected with the verb otherwise than as subject. The suffixed element in "kill-s" corresponds to the English suffix with the important exceptions that it makes no reference to the number of the subject and that the statement is known to be true, that it is vouched for by the speaker. Number is only indirectly expressed in the sentence in so far as there is no specific verb suffix indicating plurality of the subject nor specific plural elements in the two nouns. Had the statement been made on another's authority, a totally different "tense-modal" suffix would have had to be used. The pronouns of reference ("he") imply nothing by themselves as to number, gender, or case. Gender, indeed, is completely absent in Yana as a relational category.

The Yana sentence has already illustrated the point that certain of our supposedly essential concepts may be ignored; both the Yana and the German sentence illustrate the further point that certain concepts may need expression for which an English-speaking person, or rather the English-speaking habit, finds no need whatever. One could go on and give endless examples of such deviations from English form, but we shall have to content ourselves with a few more indications. In the Chinese sentence "Man kill duck," which may be looked upon as the practical equivalent of "The man kills the duck," there is by no means present for the Chinese consciousness that childish, halting, empty feeling which we experience in the literal English translation. The three concrete concepts—two objects and an action—are each directly expressed by a monosyllabic word which is at the same time a radical element; the two relational concepts—"subject" and "object"—are expressed solely by the position of the concrete words before and after the word of action. And that is all. Definiteness or indefiniteness of reference, number, personality as an inherent aspect of the verb, tense, not to speak of gender—all these are given no expression in the Chinese sentence, which, for all that, is a perfectly adequate communication —provided, of course, there is that context, that background of mutual understanding that is essential to the complete intelligibility of all speech. Nor does this qualification impair our argument, for in the English sentence too we leave unexpressed a large number of ideas which are either taken for granted or which have been developed or are about to be developed in the course of the conversation. Nothing has been said, for example, in the English, German, Yana, or Chinese sentence as to the place relations of the farmer, the duck, the speaker, and the listener. Are the farmer and the duck both visible or is one or the other invisible from the point of view of the speaker, and are both placed within the horizon of the speaker, the listener, or of some indefinite point of reference "off yonder"? In other words, to paraphrase awkwardly certain latent "demonstrative" ideas, does this farmer (invisible to us but standing behind a door not far away from me, you being seated yonder well out of reach) kill that duckling (which belongs to you)? or does that farmer (who lives in your neighborhood and whom we see over there) kill that duckling (that belongs to him)? This type of demonstrative elaboration is foreign to our way of thinking, but it would seem very natural, indeed unavoidable, to a Kwakiutl Indian.

What, then, are the absolutely essential concepts in speech, the concepts that must be expressed if language is to be a satisfactory means of communication? Clearly we must have, first of all, a large stock of basic or radical concepts, the concrete wherewithal of speech. We must have objects, actions, qualities to talk about, and these must have their corresponding symbols in independent words or in radical elements. No proposition, however abstract its intent, is humanly possible without a tying on at one or more points to the concrete world of sense. In every intelligible proposition at least two of these radical ideas must be expressed, though in exceptional cases one or even both may be understood from the context. And, secondly, such relational concepts must be expressed as moor the concrete concepts to each other and construct a definite, fundamental form of proposition. In this fundamental form there must be no doubt as to the nature of the relations that obtain between the concrete concepts. We must know what concrete concept is directly or indirectly related to what other, and how. If we wish to talk of a thing and an action, we must know if they are coördinately related to each other (e.g., "He is fond of *wine and gambling*"); or if the thing is conceived of as the starting point, the "doer" of the action, or, as it is customary to say, the "subject" of which the action is predicated; or if, on the contrary, it is the end point, the "object" of the action. If I wish to communicate an intelligible idea about a farmer, a duckling, and the act of killing, it is not enough to state the linguistic symbols for these concrete ideas in any order, higgledy-piggledy, trusting that the hearer may construct some kind of a relational pattern out of the general probabilities of the case. The fundamental syntactic relations must be unambiguously expressed. I can afford to be silent on the subject of time and place and number and of a host of other possible types of concepts, but I can find no way of dodging the issue as to who is doing the killing. There is no known language that can or does dodge it, any more than it succeeds in saying something without the use of symbols for the concrete concepts.

We are thus once more reminded of the distinction between essential or unavoidable relational concepts and the dispensable type. The former are universally expressed, the latter are but sparsely developed in some languages, elaborated with a bewildering exuberance in others. But what prevents us from throwing in these "dispensable" or "secondary" relational concepts with the large, floating group of derivational, qualifying concepts that we have already discussed? Is there, after all is said and done, a fundamental difference between a qualifying concept like the negative in *unhealthy* and a relational one like the number concept in *books*? If *unhealthy* may be roughly paraphrased as *not healthy*, may not *books* be just as legitimately paraphrased, barring the violence to English idiom, as *several book?* There are, indeed, languages in which the plural, if expressed at all, is conceived of in the same sober, restricted, one might almost say casual, spirit in which we feel the negative in *unhealthy*. For such languages the number concept has no syntactic significance whatever, is not essentially conceived of as defining a relation, but falls into the group of derivational or even of basic concepts. In English, however, as in French, German, Latin, Greek—indeed in all the languages that we have most familiarity with—the idea of number is not merely appended to a given concept of a thing. It may have something of this merely qualifying value, but its force extends far beyond. It infects much else in the sentence, molding other concepts, even such as have no intelligible relation to number, into forms that are said to correspond to or "agree with" the basic concept to which it is attached in the first instance. If "a man falls" but "men fall" in English, it is not because of any inherent change that has taken place in the nature of the action or because the idea of plurality inherent in "men" must, in the very nature of ideas, relate itself also to the action performed by these men. What we are doing in these sentences is what most languages, in greater or less degree and in a hundred varying ways, are in the habit of doing—throwing a bold bridge between the two basically distinct types of concept, the concrete and the abstractly relational, infecting the latter, as it were, with the color and grossness of the former. By a certain violence of metaphor the material concept is forced to do duty for (or intertwine itself with) the strictly relational.

The case is even more obvious if we take gender as our text. In the two English phrases, "The white woman that comes" and "The white men that come," we are not reminded that gender, as well as number, may be elevated into a secondary relational concept. It would seem a little far-fetched to make of masculinity and femininity, crassly material, philosophically accidental concepts that they are, a means of relating quality and person, person and action, nor would it easily occur to us, if we had not studied the classics, that it was anything but absurd to inject into two such highly attenuated relational concepts as are expressed by "the" and "that" the combined notions of number and sex. Yet all this, and more, happens in Latin. *Illa alba femina quae venit* and *illi albi homines qui veniunt*, conceptually translated, amount to this: *that*-one-feminine-doer [57] one-feminine-*white*-doer feminine-doing-one-*woman which*-one-feminine-doer other [58]-one-now-*come*; and: *that*-several-masculine-doer several-masculine-*white*-doer masculine-doing-several-*man which*-several-masculine-doer other-several-now-*come*. Each word involves no less than four concepts, a radical concept (either properly concrete—*white, man, woman, come*—or demonstrative—*that, which*) and three relational concepts, selected from the categories of case, number, gender, person, and tense. Logically, only case [59] (the relation of *woman* or *men* to a following verb, of *which* to its antecedent, of *that* and *white* to *woman* or *men*, and of *which* to *come*) imperatively demands expression, and that only in connection with the concepts directly affected (there is, for instance, no need to be informed that the whiteness is a doing or doer's whiteness [60]). The other relational concepts are either merely parasitic (gender throughout;

number in the demonstrative, the adjective, the relative, and the verb) or irrelevant to the essential syntactic form of the sentence (number in the noun; person; tense). An intelligent and sensitive Chinaman, accustomed as he is to cut to the very bone of linguistic form, might well say of the Latin sentence, "How pedantically imaginative!" It must be difficult for him, when first confronted by the illogical complexities of our European languages, to feel at home in an attitude that so largely confounds the subject-matter of speech with its formal pattern or, to be more accurate, that turns certain fundamentally concrete concepts to such attenuated relational uses.

I have exaggerated somewhat the concreteness of our subsidiary or rather non-syntactical relational concepts In order that the essential facts might come out in bold relief. It goes without saying that a Frenchman has no clear sex notion in his mind when he speaks of *un arbre* ("a-masculine tree") or of *une pomme* ("a-feminine apple"). Nor have we, despite the grammarians, a very vivid sense of the present as contrasted with all past and all future time when we say *He comes.* [[61]] This is evident from our use of the present to indicate both future time ("He comes to-morrow") and general activity unspecified as to time ("Whenever he comes, I am glad to see him," where "comes" refers to past occurrences and possible future ones rather than to present activity). In both the French and English instances the primary ideas of sex and time have become diluted by form-analogy and by extensions into the relational sphere, the concepts ostensibly indicated being now so vaguely delimited that it is rather the tyranny of usage than the need of their concrete expression that sways us in the selection of this or that form. If the thinning-out process continues long enough, we may eventually be left with a system of forms on our hands from which all the color of life has vanished and which merely persist by inertia, duplicating each other's secondary, syntactic functions with endless prodigality. Hence, in part, the complex conjugational systems of so many languages, in which differences of form are attended by no assignable differences of function. There must have been a time, for instance, though it antedates our earliest documentary evidence, when the type of tense formation represented by *drove* or *sank* differed in meaning, in however slightly nuanced a degree, from the type (*killed, worked*) which has now become established in English as the prevailing preterit formation, very much as we recognize a valuable distinction at present between both these types and the "perfect" (*has driven, has killed*) but may have ceased to do so at some point in the future. [[62]] Now form lives longer than its own conceptual content. Both are ceaselessly changing, but, on the whole, the form tends to linger on when the spirit has flown or changed its being. Irrational form, form for form's sake—however we term this tendency to hold on to formal distinctions once they have come to be—is as natural to the life of language as is the retention of modes of conduct that have long outlived the meaning they once had.

There is another powerful tendency which makes for a formal elaboration that does not strictly correspond to clear-cut conceptual differences. This is the tendency to construct schemes of classification into which all the concepts of language must be fitted. Once we have made up our minds that all things are either definitely good or bad or definitely black or white, it is difficult to get into the frame of mind that recognizes that any particular thing may be both good and bad (in other words, indifferent) or both black and white (in other words, gray), still more difficult to realize that the good-bad or black-white categories may not apply at all. Language is in many respects as unreasonable and stubborn about its classifications as is such a mind. It must have its perfectly exclusive pigeon-holes and will tolerate no flying vagrants. Any concept that asks for expression must submit to the classificatory rules of the game, just as there are statistical surveys in which even the most convinced atheist must perforce be labeled Catholic, Protestant, or Jew or get no hearing. In English we have made up our minds that all action must be conceived of in reference to three standard times. If, therefore, we desire to state a proposition that is as true to-morrow as it was yesterday, we have to pretend that the present moment may be elongated fore and aft so as to take in all eternity. [[63]] In French we know once for all that an object is masculine or feminine, whether it be living or not; just as in many American and East Asiatic languages it must be understood to belong to a certain form-category (say, ring-round, ball-round, long and slender, cylindrical, sheet-like, in mass like sugar) before it can be enumerated (e.g., "two ball-class potatoes," "three sheet-class carpets") or even said to "be" or "be handled in a definite way" (thus, in the Athabaskan languages and in Yana, "to carry" or "throw" a pebble is quite another thing than to carry or throw a log, linguistically no less than in terms of muscular experience). Such instances might be multiplied at will. It is almost as though at some period in the past the unconscious mind of the race had made a hasty inventory of experience, committed itself to a premature classification that allowed of no revision, and saddled the inheritors of its language with a science that they no longer quite believed in nor had the strength to overthrow. Dogma, rigidly prescribed by tradition, stiffens into formalism. Linguistic categories make up a system of surviving dogma—dogma of the unconscious. They are often but half real as concepts; their life tends ever to languish away into form for form's sake.

There is still a third cause for the rise of this non-significant form, or rather of non-significant differences of form. This is the mechanical operation of phonetic processes, which may bring about formal distinctions that have not and never had a corresponding functional distinction. Much of the irregularity and general formal complexity of our declensional and conjugational systems is due to this process. The plural of *hat* is *hats*, the plural of *self* is *selves*. In the former case we have a true -*s* symbolizing plurality, in the latter a *z*-sound coupled with a change in the radical element of the word of *f* to *v*. Here we have not a falling together of forms that originally stood for fairly distinct concepts—as we saw was presumably the case with such parallel forms as *drove* and *worked*—but a merely mechanical manifolding of the same formal element without a corresponding growth of a new concept. This type of form development, therefore, while of the greatest interest for the general history of language, does not directly concern us now in our effort to understand the nature of grammatical concepts and their tendency to degenerate into purely formal counters.

We may now conveniently revise our first classification of concepts as expressed in language and suggest the following scheme:

I. *Basic (Concrete) Concepts* (such as objects, actions, qualities): normally expressed by independent words or radical elements; involve no relation as such [64]

II. *Derivational Concepts* (less concrete, as a rule, than I, more so than III): normally expressed by affixing non-radical elements to radical elements or by inner modification of these; differ from type I in defining ideas that are irrelevant to the proposition as a whole but that give a radical element a particular increment of significance and that are thus inherently related in a specific way to concepts of type I [65]

III. *Concrete Relational Concepts* (still more abstract, yet not entirely devoid of a measure of concreteness): normally expressed by affixing non-radical elements to radical elements, but generally at a greater remove from these than is the case with elements of type II, or by inner modification of radical elements; differ fundamentally from type II in indicating or implying relations that transcend the particular word to which they are immediately attached, thus leading over to

IV. *Pure Relational Concepts* (purely abstract): normally expressed by affixing non-radical elements to radical elements (in which case these concepts are frequently intertwined with those of type III) or by their inner modification, by independent words, or by position; serve to relate the concrete elements of the proposition to each other, thus giving it definite syntactic form.

The nature of these four classes of concepts as regards their concreteness or their power to express syntactic relations may be thus symbolized:

Material Content $\begin{cases} \text{I. Basic Concepts} \\ \text{II. Derivational Concepts} \end{cases}$

Relation $\begin{cases} \text{III. Concrete Relational Concepts} \\ \text{IV. Pure Relational Concepts} \end{cases}$

These schemes must not be worshipped as fetiches. In the actual work of analysis difficult problems frequently arise and we may well be in doubt as to how to group a given set of concepts. This is particularly apt to be the case in exotic languages, where we may be quite sure of the analysis of the words in a sentence and yet not succeed in acquiring that inner "feel" of its structure that enables us to tell infallibly what is "material content" and what is "relation." Concepts of class I are essential to all speech, also concepts of class IV. Concepts II and III are both common, but not essential; particularly group III, which represents, in effect, a psychological and formal confusion of types II and IV or of types I and IV, is an avoidable class of concepts. Logically there is an impassable gulf between I and IV, but the illogical, metaphorical genius of speech has wilfully spanned the gulf and set up a continuous gamut of concepts and forms that leads imperceptibly from the crudest of materialities ("house" or "John Smith") to the most subtle of relations. It is particularly significant that the unanalyzable independent word belongs in most cases to either group I or group IV, rather less commonly to II or III. It is possible for a concrete concept, represented by a simple word, to lose its material significance entirely and pass over directly into the relational sphere without at the same time losing its independence as a word. This happens, for instance, in Chinese and Cambodgian when the verb "give" is used in an abstract sense as a mere symbol of the "indirect objective" relation (e.g., Cambodgian "We make story this give all that person who have child," i.e., "We have made this story *for* all those that have children").

There are, of course, also not a few instances of transitions between groups I and II and I and III, as well as of the less radical one between II and III. To the first of these transitions belongs that whole class of examples in which the independent word, after passing through the preliminary stage of functioning as the secondary or qualifying element in a compound, ends up by being a derivational affix pure and simple, yet without losing the memory of its former independence. Such an element and concept is the *full* of *teaspoonfull*, which hovers psychologically between the status of an independent, radical concept (compare *full*) or of a subsidiary element in a compound (cf. *brim-full*) and that of a simple suffix (cf. *dutiful*) in which the primary concreteness is no longer felt. In general, the more highly synthetic our linguistic type, the more difficult and even arbitrary it becomes to distinguish groups I and II.

Not only is there a gradual loss of the concrete as we pass through from group I to group IV, there is also a constant fading away of the feeling of sensible reality within the main groups of linguistic concepts themselves. In many languages it becomes almost imperative, therefore, to make various sub-classifications, to segregate, for instance, the more concrete from the more abstract concepts of group II. Yet we must always beware of reading into such abstracter groups that purely formal, relational feeling that we can hardly help associating with certain of the abstracter concepts which, with us, fall in group III, unless, indeed, there is clear evidence to warrant such a reading in. An example or two should make clear these all-important distinctions. [66] In Nootka we have an unusually large number of derivational affixes (expressing concepts of group II). Some of these are quite material in content (e.g., "in the house," "to dream of"), others, like an element denoting plurality and a diminutive affix, are far more abstract in content. The former type are more closely welded with the radical element than the latter, which can only be suffixed to formations that have the value of complete words. If, therefore, I wish to say "the small fires in the house"—and I can do this in one word—I must form the word "fire-in-the-house," to which elements corresponding to "small," our plural, and "the" are appended. The element indicating the definiteness of reference that is implied in our "the" comes at the very end of the word. So far, so good. "Fire-in-the-house-the" is an intelligible correlate of our "the house-fire."[67] But is the Nootka correlate of "the small fires in the house" the true equivalent of an English "*the house-firelets*"?[68] By no means. First of all, the plural element precedes the diminutive in Nootka: "fire-in-the-house-plural-small-the," in other words "the house-fires-let," which at once reveals the important fact that the plural concept is not as abstractly, as relationally, felt as in English. A more adequate rendering would be "the house-fire-several-let," in which, however, "several" is too gross a word, "-let" too choice an element ("small" again is too gross). In truth we cannot carry over into English the inherent feeling of the Nootka word, which seems to hover somewhere between "the house-firelets" and "the house-fire-several-small." But what more than anything else cuts off all possibility of comparison between the English -*s* of "house-firelets" and the "-several-small" of the Nootka word is this, that in Nootka neither the plural nor the diminutive affix corresponds or refers to anything else in the sentence. In English "the house-firelets burn" (not "burns"), in Nootka neither verb, nor adjective, nor anything else in the proposition is in the least concerned with the plurality or the diminutiveness of the fire. Hence, while Nootka recognizes a cleavage between concrete and less concrete concepts within group II, the less concrete do not transcend the group and lead us into that abstracter air into which our plural -*s* carries us. But at any rate, the reader may object, it is something that the Nootka plural affix is set apart from the concreter group of affixes; and may not the Nootka diminutive have a slenderer, a more elusive content than our -*let* or -*ling* or the German -*chen* or -*lein?*[69]

Can such a concept as that of plurality ever be classified with the more material concepts of group II? Indeed it can be. In Yana the third person of the verb makes no formal distinction between singular and plural. Nevertheless the plural concept can be, and nearly always is, expressed by the suffixing of an element (-*ba*-) to the radical element of the verb. "It burns in the east" is rendered by the verb *ya-hau-si* "burn-east-s."[70]

"They burn in the east" is *ya-ba-hau-si*. Note that the plural affix immediately follows the radical element (*ya-*), disconnecting it from the local element (*-hau-*). It needs no labored argument to prove that the concept of plurality is here hardly less concrete than that of location "in the east," and that the Yana form corresponds in feeling not so much to our "They burn in the east" (*ardunt oriente*) as to a "Burn-several-east-s, it plurally burns in the east," an expression which we cannot adequately assimilate for lack of the necessary form-grooves into which to run it.

But can we go a step farther and dispose of the category of plurality as an utterly material idea, one that would make of "books" a "plural book," in which the "plural," like the "white" of "white book," falls contentedly into group I? Our "many books" and "several books" are obviously not cases in point. Even if we could say "many book" and "several book" (as we can say "many a book" and "each book"), the plural concept would still not emerge as clearly as it should for our argument; "many" and "several" are contaminated by certain notions of quantity or scale that are not essential to the idea of plurality itself. We must turn to central and eastern Asia for the type of expression we are seeking. In Tibetan, for instance, *nga-s mi mthong*[71] "I-by man see, by me a man is seen, I see a man" may just as well be understood to mean "I see men," if there happens to be no reason to emphasize the fact of plurality.[72] If the fact is worth expressing, however, I can say *nga-s mi rnams mthong* "by me man plural see," where *rnams* is the perfect conceptual analogue of *-s* in *books*, divested of all relational strings. *Rnams* follows its noun as would any other attributive word—"man plural" (whether two or a million) like "man white." No need to bother about his plurality any more than about his whiteness unless we insist on the point.

What is true of the idea of plurality is naturally just as true of a great many other concepts. They do not necessarily belong where we who speak English are in the habit of putting them. They may be shifted towards I or towards IV, the two poles of linguistic expression. Nor dare we look down on the Nootka Indian and the Tibetan for their material attitude towards a concept which to us is abstract and relational, lest we invite the reproaches of the Frenchman who feels a subtlety of relation in *femme blanche* and *homme blanc* that he misses in the coarser-grained *white woman* and *white man*. But the Bantu Negro, were he a philosopher, might go further and find it strange that we put in group II a category, the diminutive, which he strongly feels to belong to group III and which he uses, along with a number of other classificatory concepts,[73] to relate his subjects and objects, attributes and predicates, as a Russian or a German handles his genders and, if possible, with an even greater finesse.

It is because our conceptual scheme is a sliding scale rather than a philosophical analysis of experience that we cannot say in advance just where to put a given concept. We must dispense, in other words, with a well-ordered classification of categories. What boots it to put tense and mode here or number there when the next language one handles puts tense a peg "lower down" (towards I), mode and number a peg "higher up" (towards IV)? Nor is there much to be gained in a summary work of this kind from a general inventory of the types of concepts generally found in groups II, III, and IV. There are too many possibilities. It would be interesting to show what are the most typical noun-forming and verb-forming elements of group II; how variously nouns may be classified (by gender; personal and non-personal; animate and inanimate; by form; common and proper); how the concept of number is elaborated (singular and plural; singular, dual, and plural; singular, dual, trial, and plural; single, distributive, and collective); what tense distinctions may be made in verb or noun (the "past," for instance, may be an indefinite past, immediate, remote, mythical, completed, prior); how delicately certain languages have developed the idea of "aspect"[74] (momentaneous, durative, continuative, inceptive, cessative, durative-inceptive, iterative, momentaneous-iterative, durative-iterative, resultative, and still others); what modalities may be recognized (indicative, imperative, potential, dubitative, optative, negative, and a host of others[75]); what distinctions of person are possible (is "we," for instance, conceived of as a plurality of "I" or is it as distinct from "I" as either is from "you" or "he"?—both attitudes are illustrated in language; moreover, does "we" include you to whom I speak or not?—"inclusive" and "exclusive" forms); what may be the general scheme of orientation, the so-called demonstrative categories ("this" and "that" in an endless procession of nuances);[76] how frequently the form expresses the source or nature of the speaker's knowledge (known by actual experience, by hearsay,[77] by inference); how the syntactic relations may be expressed in the noun (subjective and objective; agentive, instrumental, and person affected;[78] various types of "genitive" and indirect relations) and, correspondingly, in the verb (active and passive; active and static; transitive and intransitive;

impersonal, reflexive, reciprocal, indefinite as to object, and many other special limitations on the starting-point and end-point of the flow of activity). These details, important as many of them are to an understanding of the "inner form" of language, yield in general significance to the more radical group-distinctions that we have set up. It is enough for the general reader to feel that language struggles towards two poles of linguistic expression—material content and relation—and that these poles tend to be connected by a long series of transitional concepts.

In dealing with words and their varying forms we have had to anticipate much that concerns the sentence as a whole. Every language has its special method or methods of binding words into a larger unity. The importance of these methods is apt to vary with the complexity of the individual word. The more synthetic the language, in other words, the more clearly the status of each word in the sentence is indicated by its own resources, the less need is there for looking beyond the word to the sentence as a whole. The Latin *agit* "(he) acts" needs no outside help to establish its place in a proposition. Whether I say *agit dominus* "the master acts" or *sic femina agit* "thus the woman acts," the net result as to the syntactic feel of the *agit* is practically the same. It can only be a verb, the predicate of a proposition, and it can only be conceived as a statement of activity carried out by a person (or thing) other than you or me. It is not so with such a word as the English *act*. *Act* is a syntactic waif until we have defined its status in a proposition—one thing in "they act abominably," quite another in "that was a kindly act." The Latin sentence speaks with the assurance of its individual members, the English word needs the prompting of its fellows. Roughly speaking, to be sure. And yet to say that a sufficiently elaborate word-structure compensates for external syntactic methods is perilously close to begging the question. The elements of the word are related to each other in a specific way and follow each other in a rigorously determined sequence. This is tantamount to saying that a word which consists of more than a radical element is a crystallization of a sentence or of some portion of a sentence, that a form like *agit* is roughly the psychological equivalent of a form like *age is* "act he." Breaking down, then, the wall that separates word and sentence, we may ask: What, at last analysis, are the fundamental methods of relating word to word and element to element, in short, of passing from the isolated notions symbolized by each word and by each element to the unified proposition that corresponds to a thought?

    The answer is simple and is implied in the preceding remarks. The most fundamental and the most powerful of all relating methods is the method of order. Let us think of some more or less concrete idea, say a color, and set down its symbol—*red*; of another concrete idea, say a person or object, setting down its symbol—*dog*; finally, of a third concrete idea, say an action, setting down its symbol—*run*. It is hardly possible to set down these three symbols—*red dog run*—without relating them in some way, for example *(the) red dog run(s)*. I am far from wishing to state that the proposition has always grown up in this analytic manner, merely that the very process of juxtaposing concept to concept, symbol to symbol, forces some kind of relational "feeling," if nothing else, upon us. To certain syntactic adhesions we are very sensitive, for example, to the attributive relation of quality (*red dog*) or the subjective relation (*dog run*) or the objective relation (*kill dog*), to others we are more indifferent, for example, to the attributive relation of circumstance (*to-day red dog run* or *red dog to-day run* or *red dog run to-day*, all of which are equivalent propositions or propositions in embryo). Words and elements, then, once they are listed in a certain order, tend not only to establish some kind of relation among themselves but are attracted to each other in greater or in less degree. It is presumably this very greater or less that ultimately leads to those firmly solidified groups of elements (radical element or elements plus one or more grammatical elements) that we have studied as complex words. They are in all likelihood nothing but sequences that have shrunk together and away from other sequences or isolated elements in the flow of speech. While they are fully alive, in other words, while they are functional at every point, they can keep themselves at a psychological distance from their neighbors. As they gradually lose much of their life, they fall back into the embrace of the sentence as a whole and the sequence of independent words regains the importance it had in part transferred to the crystallized groups of elements. Speech is thus constantly tightening and loosening its sequences. In its highly integrated forms (Latin, Eskimo) the "energy" of sequence is largely locked up in complex word formations, it becomes transformed into a kind of potential energy that may not be released for millennia. In its more analytic forms (Chinese, English) this energy is mobile, ready to hand for such service as we demand of it.

There can be little doubt that stress has frequently played a controlling influence in the formation of element-groups or complex words out of certain sequences in the sentence. Such an English word as *withstand* is merely an old sequence *with stand*, i.e., "against stand," in which the unstressed adverb was permanently drawn to the following verb and lost its independence as a significant element. In the same way French futures of the type *irai* "(I) shall go" are but the resultants of a coalescence of originally independent words: *ir a'i* "to-go I-have," under the influence of a unifying accent. But stress has done more than articulate or unify sequences that in their own right imply a syntactic relation. Stress is the most natural means at our disposal to emphasize a linguistic contrast, to indicate the major element in a sequence. Hence we need not be surprised to find that accent too, no less than sequence, may serve as the unaided symbol of certain relations. Such a contrast as that of *go' between* ("one who goes between") and *to go between'* may be of quite secondary origin in English, but there is every reason to believe that analogous distinctions have prevailed at all times in linguistic history. A sequence like *see' man* might imply some type of relation in which *see* qualifies the following word, hence "a seeing man" or "a seen (or visible) man," or is its predication, hence "the man sees" or "the man is seen," while a sequence like *see man'* might indicate that the accented word in some way limits the application of the first, say as direct object, hence "to see a man" or "(he) sees the man." Such alternations of relation, as symbolized by varying stresses, are important and frequent in a number of languages.

It is a somewhat venturesome and yet not an altogether unreasonable speculation that sees in word order and stress the primary methods for the expression of all syntactic relations and looks upon the present relational value of specific words and elements as but a secondary condition due to a transfer of values. Thus, we may surmise that the Latin *-m* of words like *feminam, dominum,* and *civem* did not originally denote that "woman," "master," and "citizen" were objectively related to the verb of the proposition but indicated something far more concrete, that the objective relation was merely implied by the position or accent of the word (radical element) immediately preceding the *-m*, and that gradually, as its more concrete significance faded away, it took over a syntactic function that did not originally belong to it. This sort of evolution by transfer is traceable in many instances. Thus, the *of* in an English phrase like "the law of the land" is now as colorless in content, as purely a relational indicator as the "genitive" suffix *-is* in the Latin *lex urbis* "the law of the city." We know, however, that it was originally an adverb of considerable concreteness of meaning,[85] "away, moving from," and that the syntactic relation was originally expressed by the case form [86] of the second noun. As the case form lost its vitality, the adverb took over its function. If we are actually justified in assuming that the expression of all syntactic relations is ultimately traceable to these two unavoidable, dynamic features of speech —sequence and stress [87]—an interesting thesis results:—All of the actual content of speech, its clusters of vocalic and consonantal sounds, is in origin limited to the concrete; relations were originally not expressed in outward form but were merely implied and articulated with the help of order and rhythm. In other words, relations were intuitively felt and could only "leak out" with the help of dynamic factors that themselves move on an intuitional plane.

There is a special method for the expression of relations that has been so often evolved in the history of language that we must glance at it for a moment. This is the method of "concord" or of like signaling. It is based on the same principle as the password or label. All persons or objects that answer to the same counter-sign or that bear the same imprint are thereby stamped as somehow related. It makes little difference, once they are so stamped, where they are to be found or how they behave themselves. They are known to belong together. We are familiar with the principle of concord in Latin and Greek. Many of us have been struck by such relentless rhymes as *vidi ilium bonum dominum* "I saw that good master" or *quarum dearum saevarum* "of which stern goddesses." Not that sound-echo, whether in the form of rhyme or of alliteration [88] is necessary to concord, though in its most typical and original forms concord is nearly always accompanied by sound repetition. The essence of the principle is simply this, that words (elements) that belong together, particularly if they are syntactic equivalents or are related in like fashion to another word or element, are outwardly marked by the same or functionally equivalent affixes. The application of the principle varies considerably according to the genius of the particular language. In Latin and Greek, for instance, there is concord between noun and qualifying word (adjective or demonstrative) as regards gender, number, and case, between verb and subject only as regards number, and no concord between verb and object.

In Chinook there is a more far-reaching concord between noun, whether subject or object, and verb. Every noun is classified according to five categories—masculine, feminine, neuter,[89] dual, and plural. "Woman" is feminine, "sand" is neuter, "table" is masculine. If, therefore, I wish to say "The woman put the sand on the table," I must place in the verb certain class or gender prefixes that accord with corresponding noun prefixes. The sentence reads then, "The (fem.)-woman she (fem.)-it (neut.)-it (masc.)-on-put the (neut.)-sand the (masc.)-table." If "sand" is qualified as "much" and "table" as "large," these new ideas are expressed as abstract nouns, each with its inherent class-prefix ("much" is neuter or feminine, "large" is masculine) and with a possessive prefix referring to the qualified noun. Adjective thus calls to noun, noun to verb. "The woman put much sand on the large table," therefore, takes the form: "The (fem.)-woman she (fem.)-it (neut.)-it (masc.)-on-put the (fem.)-thereof (neut.)-quantity the (neut.)-sand the (masc.)-thereof (masc.)-largeness the (masc.)-table." The classification of "table" as masculine is thus three times insisted on—in the noun, in the adjective, and in the verb. In the Bantu languages,[90] the principle of concord works very much as in Chinook. In them also nouns are classified into a number of categories and are brought into relation with adjectives, demonstratives, relative pronouns, and verbs by means of prefixed elements that call off the class and make up a complex system of concordances. In such a sentence as "That fierce lion who came here is dead," the class of "lion," which we may call the animal class, would be referred to by concording prefixes no less than six times,—with the demonstrative ("that"), the qualifying adjective, the noun itself, the relative pronoun, the subjective prefix to the verb of the relative clause, and the subjective prefix to the verb of the main clause ("is dead"). We recognize in this insistence on external clarity of reference the same spirit as moves in the more familiar *illum bonum dominum*.

Psychologically the methods of sequence and accent lie at the opposite pole to that of concord. Where they are all for implication, for subtlety of feeling, concord is impatient of the least ambiguity but must have its well-certificated tags at every turn. Concord tends to dispense with order. In Latin and Chinook the independent words are free in position, less so in Bantu. In both Chinook and Bantu, however, the methods of concord and order are equally important for the differentiation of subject and object, as the classifying verb prefixes refer to subject, object, or indirect object according to the relative position they occupy. These examples again bring home to us the significant fact that at some point or other order asserts itself in every language as the most fundamental of relating principles.

The observant reader has probably been surprised that all this time we have had so little to say of the time-honored "parts of speech." The reason for this is not far to seek. Our conventional classification of words into parts of speech is only a vague, wavering approximation to a consistently worked out inventory of experience. We imagine, to begin with, that all "verbs" are inherently concerned with action as such, that a "noun" is the name of some definite object or personality that can be pictured by the mind, that all qualities are necessarily expressed by a definite group of words to which we may appropriately apply the term "adjective." As soon as we test our vocabulary, we discover that the parts of speech are far from corresponding to so simple an analysis of reality. We say "it is red" and define "red" as a quality-word or adjective. We should consider it strange to think of an equivalent of "is red" in which the whole predication (adjective and verb of being) is conceived of as a verb in precisely the same way in which we think of "extends" or "lies" or "sleeps" as a verb. Yet as soon as we give the "durative" notion of being red an inceptive or transitional turn, we can avoid the parallel form "it becomes red, it turns red" and say "it reddens." No one denies that "reddens" is as good a verb as "sleeps" or even "walks." Yet "it is red" is related to "it reddens" very much as is "he stands" to "he stands up" or "he rises." It is merely a matter of English or of general Indo-European idiom that we cannot say "it reds" in the sense of "it is red." There are hundreds of languages that can. Indeed there are many that can express what we should call an adjective only by making a participle out of a verb. "Red" in such languages is merely a derivative "being red," as our "sleeping" or "walking" are derivatives of primary verbs.

Just as we can verbify the idea of a quality in such cases as "reddens," so we can represent a quality or an action to ourselves as a thing. We speak of "the height of a building" or "the fall of an apple" quite as though these ideas were parallel to "the roof of a building" or "the skin of an apple," forgetting that the nouns (*height, fall*) have not ceased to indicate a quality and an act when we have made them speak with the accent of mere objects. And just as there are languages that make verbs of the great mass of adjectives, so there are others that make nouns of them. In Chinook, as we have seen, "the big table" is "the-table its-bigness"; in Tibetan the same idea may be expressed by "the table of bigness," very much as we may say "a man of wealth" instead of "a rich man."

But are there not certain ideas that it is impossible to render except by way of such and such parts of speech? What can be done with the "to" of "he came to the house"? Well, we can say "he reached the house" and dodge the preposition altogether, giving the verb a nuance that absorbs the idea of local relation carried by the "to." But let us insist on giving independence to this idea of local relation. Must we not then hold to the preposition? No, we can make a noun of it. We can say something like "he reached the proximity of the house" or "he reached the house-locality." Instead of saying "he looked into the glass" we may say "he scrutinized the glass-interior." Such expressions are stilted in English because they do not easily fit into our formal grooves, but in language after language we find that local relations are expressed in just this way. The local relation is nominalized. And so we might go on examining the various parts of speech and showing how they not merely grade into each other but are to an astonishing degree actually convertible into each other. The upshot of such an examination would be to feel convinced that the "part of speech" reflects not so much our intuitive analysis of reality as our ability to compose that reality into a variety of formal patterns. A part of speech outside of the limitations of syntactic form is but a will o' the wisp. For this reason no logical scheme of the parts of speech—their number, nature, and necessary confines—is of the slightest interest to the linguist. Each language has its own scheme. Everything depends on the formal demarcations which it recognizes.

Yet we must not be too destructive. It is well to remember that speech consists of a series of propositions. There must be something to talk about and something must be said about this subject of discourse once it is selected. This distinction is of such fundamental importance that the vast majority of languages have emphasized it by creating some sort of formal barrier between the two terms of the proposition. The subject of discourse is a noun. As the most common subject of discourse is either a person or a thing, the noun clusters about concrete concepts of that order. As the thing predicated of a subject is generally an activity in the widest sense of the word, a passage from one moment of existence to another, the form which has been set aside for the business of predicating, in other words, the verb, clusters about concepts of activity. No language wholly fails to distinguish noun and verb, though in particular cases the nature of the distinction may be an elusive one. It is different with the other parts of speech. Not one of them is imperatively required for the life of language. [[91]]

Types of Linguistic Structure

So far, in dealing with linguistic form, we have been concerned only with single words and with the relations of words in sentences. We have not envisaged whole languages as conforming to this or that general type. Incidentally we have observed that one language runs to tight-knit synthesis where another contents itself with a more analytic, piece-meal handling of its elements, or that in one language syntactic relations appear pure which in another are combined with certain other notions that have something concrete about them, however abstract they may be felt to be in practice. In this way we may have obtained some inkling of what is meant when we speak of the general form of a language. For it must be obvious to any one who has thought about the question at all or who has felt something of the spirit of a foreign language that there is such a thing as a basic plan, a certain cut, to each language. This type or plan or structural "genius" of the language is something much more fundamental, much more pervasive, than any single feature of it that we can mention, nor can we gain an adequate idea of its nature by a mere recital of the sundry facts that make up the grammar of the language. When we pass from Latin to Russian, we feel that it is approximately the same horizon that bounds our view, even though the near, familiar landmarks have changed. When we come to English, we seem to notice that the hills have dipped down a little, yet we recognize the general lay of the land. And when we have arrived at Chinese, it is an utterly different sky that is looking down upon us. We can translate these metaphors and say that all languages differ from one another but that certain ones differ far more than others. This is tantamount to saying that it is possible to group them into morphological types.

Strictly speaking, we know in advance that it is impossible to set up a limited number of types that would do full justice to the peculiarities of the thousands of languages and dialects spoken on the surface of the earth. Like all human institutions, speech is too variable and too elusive to be quite safely ticketed. Even if we operate with a minutely subdivided scale of types, we may be quite certain that many of our languages will need trimming before they fit. To get them into the scheme at all it will be necessary to overestimate the significance of this or that feature or to ignore, for the time being, certain contradictions in their mechanism. Does the difficulty of classification prove the uselessness of the task? I do not think so. It would be too easy to relieve ourselves of the burden of constructive thinking and to take the standpoint that each language has its unique history, therefore its unique structure. Such a standpoint expresses only a half truth. Just as similar social, economic, and religious institutions have grown up in different parts of the world from distinct historical antecedents, so also languages, traveling along different roads, have tended to converge toward similar forms. Moreover, the historical study of language has proven to us beyond all doubt that a language changes not only gradually but consistently, that it moves unconsciously from one type towards another, and that analogous trends are observable in remote quarters of the globe. From this it follows that broadly similar morphologies must have been reached by unrelated languages, independently and frequently. In assuming the existence of comparable types, therefore, we are not gainsaying the individuality of all historical processes; we are merely affirming that back of the face of history are powerful drifts that move language, like other social products, to balanced patterns, in other words, to types. As linguists we shall be content to realize that there are these types and that certain processes in the life of language tend to modify them. Why similar types should be formed, just what is the nature of the forces that make them and dissolve them—these questions are more easily asked than answered. Perhaps the psychologists of the future will be able to give us the ultimate reasons for the formation of linguistic types.

When it comes to the actual task of classification, we find that we have no easy road to travel. Various classifications have been suggested, and they all contain elements of value. Yet none proves satisfactory. They do not so much enfold the known languages in their embrace as force them down into narrow, straight-backed seats. The difficulties have been of various kinds. First and foremost, it has been difficult to choose a point of view. On what basis shall we classify? A language shows us so many facets that we may well be puzzled. And is one point of view sufficient? Secondly, it is dangerous to generalize from a small number of selected languages. To take, as the sum total of our material, Latin, Arabic, Turkish, Chinese, and perhaps Eskimo or Sioux as an afterthought, is to court disaster. We have no right to assume that a sprinkling of exotic types will do to supplement the few languages nearer home that we are more immediately interested in. Thirdly, the strong craving for a simple formula has been the undoing of linguists. There is something irresistible about a method of classification that starts with two poles, exemplified, say, by Chinese and Latin, clusters what it conveniently can about these poles, and throws everything else into a "transitional type." Hence has arisen the still popular classification of languages into an "isolating" group, an "agglutinative" group, and an "inflective" group. Sometimes the languages of the American Indians are made to straggle along as an uncomfortable "polysynthetic" rear-guard to the agglutinative languages. There is justification for the use of all of these terms, though not perhaps in quite the spirit in which they are commonly employed. In any case it is very difficult to assign all known languages to one or other of these groups, the more so as they are not mutually exclusive. A language may be both agglutinative and inflective, or inflective and polysynthetic, or even polysynthetic and isolating, as we shall see a little later on.

There is a fourth reason why the classification of languages has generally proved a fruitless undertaking. It is probably the most powerful deterrent of all to clear thinking. This is the evolutionary prejudice which instilled itself into the social sciences towards the middle of the last century and which is only now beginning to abate its tyrannical hold on our mind. Intermingled with this scientific prejudice and largely anticipating it was another, a more human one. The vast majority of linguistic theorists themselves spoke languages of a certain type, of which the most fully developed varieties were the Latin and Greek that they had learned in their childhood. It was not difficult for them to be persuaded that these familiar languages represented the "highest" development that speech had yet attained and that all other types were but steps on the way to this beloved "inflective" type. Whatever conformed to the pattern of Sanskrit and Greek and Latin and German was accepted as expressive of the "highest," whatever departed from it was frowned upon as a shortcoming or was at best an interesting aberration. Now any classification that starts with preconceived values or that works up to sentimental satisfactions is self-condemned as unscientific. A linguist that insists on talking about the Latin type of morphology as though it were necessarily the high-water mark of linguistic development is like the zoölogist that sees in the organic world a huge conspiracy to evolve the race-horse or the Jersey cow. Language in its fundamental forms is the symbolic expression of human intuitions. These may shape themselves in a hundred ways, regardless of the material advancement or backwardness of the people that handle the forms, of which, it need hardly be said, they are in the main unconscious. If, therefore, we wish to understand language in its true inwardness we must disabuse our minds of preferred "values"[94] and accustom ourselves to look upon English and Hottentot with the same cool, yet interested, detachment.

We come back to our first difficulty. What point of view shall we adopt for our classification? After all that we have said about grammatical form in the preceding chapter, it is clear that we cannot now make the distinction between form languages and formless languages that used to appeal to some of the older writers. Every language can and must express the fundamental syntactic relations even though there is not a single affix to be found in its vocabulary. We conclude that every language is a form language. Aside from the expression of pure relation a language may, of course, be "formless"—formless, that is, in the mechanical and rather superficial sense that it is not encumbered by the use of non-radical elements. The attempt has sometimes been made to formulate a distinction on the basis of "inner form." Chinese, for instance, has no formal elements pure and simple, no "outer form," but it evidences a keen sense of relations, of the difference between subject and object, attribute and predicate, and so on. In other words, it has an "inner form" in the same sense in which Latin possesses it, though it is outwardly "formless" where Latin is outwardly "formal." On the other hand, there are supposed to be languages[95] which have no true grasp of the fundamental relations but content themselves with the more or less minute expression of material ideas, sometimes with an exuberant display of "outer form," leaving the pure relations to be merely inferred from the context. I am strongly inclined to believe that this supposed "inner formlessness" of certain languages is an illusion. It may well be that in these languages the relations are not expressed in as immaterial a way as in Chinese or even as in Latin,[96] or that the principle of order is subject to greater fluctuations than in Chinese, or that a tendency to complex derivations relieves the language of the necessity of expressing certain relations as explicitly as a more analytic language would have them expressed.[97] All this does not mean that the languages in question have not a true feeling for the fundamental relations. We shall therefore not be able to use the notion of "inner formlessness," except in the greatly modified sense that syntactic relations may be fused with notions of another order. To this criterion of classification we shall have to return a little later.

More justifiable would be a classification according to the formal processes [[98]] most typically developed in the language. Those languages that always identify the word with the radical element would be set off as an "isolating" group against such as either affix modifying elements (affixing languages) or possess the power to change the significance of the radical element by internal changes (reduplication; vocalic and consonantal change; changes in quantity, stress, and pitch). The latter type might be not inaptly termed "symbolic" languages. [[99]] The affixing languages would naturally subdivide themselves into such as are prevailingly prefixing, like Bantu or Tlingit, and such as are mainly or entirely suffixing, like Eskimo or Algonkin or Latin. There are two serious difficulties with this fourfold classification (isolating, prefixing, suffixing, symbolic). In the first place, most languages fall into more than one of these groups. The Semitic languages, for instance, are prefixing, suffixing, and symbolic at one and the same time. In the second place, the classification in its bare form is superficial. It would throw together languages that differ utterly in spirit merely because of a certain external formal resemblance. There is clearly a world of difference between a prefixing language like Cambodgian, which limits itself, so far as its prefixes (and infixes) are concerned, to the expression of derivational concepts, and the Bantu languages, in which the prefixed elements have a far-reaching significance as symbols of syntactic relations. The classification has much greater value if it is taken to refer to the expression of relational concepts [[100]] alone. In this modified form we shall return to it as a subsidiary criterion. We shall find that the terms "isolating," "affixing," and "symbolic" have a real value. But instead of distinguishing between prefixing and suffixing languages, we shall find that it is of superior interest to make another distinction, one that is based on the relative firmness with which the affixed elements are united with the core of the word. [[101]]

There is another very useful set of distinctions that can be made, but these too must not be applied exclusively, or our classification will again be superficial. I refer to the notions of "analytic," "synthetic," and "polysynthetic." The terms explain themselves. An analytic language is one that either does not combine concepts into single words at all (Chinese) or does so economically (English, French). In an analytic language the sentence is always of prime importance, the word is of minor interest. In a synthetic language (Latin, Arabic, Finnish) the concepts cluster more thickly, the words are more richly chambered, but there is a tendency, on the whole, to keep the range of concrete significance in the single word down to a moderate compass. A polysynthetic language, as its name implies, is more than ordinarily synthetic. The elaboration of the word is extreme. Concepts which we should never dream of treating in a subordinate fashion are symbolized by derivational affixes or "symbolic" changes in the radical element, while the more abstract notions, including the syntactic relations, may also be conveyed by the word. A polysynthetic language illustrates no principles that are not already exemplified in the more familiar synthetic languages. It is related to them very much as a synthetic language is related to our own analytic English.[102] The three terms are purely quantitative—and relative, that is, a language may be "analytic" from one standpoint, "synthetic" from another. I believe the terms are more useful in defining certain drifts than as absolute counters. It is often illuminating to point out that a language has been becoming more and more analytic in the course of its history or that it shows signs of having crystallized from a simple analytic base into a highly synthetic form.[103]

We now come to the difference between an "inflective" and an "agglutinative" language. As I have already remarked, the distinction is a useful, even a necessary, one, but it has been generally obscured by a number of irrelevancies and by the unavailing effort to make the terms cover all languages that are not, like Chinese, of a definitely isolating cast. The meaning that we had best assign to the term "inflective" can be gained by considering very briefly what are some of the basic features of Latin and Greek that have been looked upon as peculiar to the inflective languages. First of all, they are synthetic rather than analytic. This does not help us much. Relatively to many another language that resembles them in broad structural respects, Latin and Greek are not notably synthetic; on the other hand, their modern descendants, Italian and Modern Greek, while far more analytic [104] than they, have not departed so widely in structural outlines as to warrant their being put in a distinct major group. An inflective language, we must insist, may be analytic, synthetic, or polysynthetic.

Latin and Greek are mainly affixing in their method, with the emphasis heavily on suffixing. The agglutinative languages are just as typically affixing as they, some among them favoring prefixes, others running to the use of suffixes. Affixing alone does not define inflection. Possibly everything depends on just what kind of affixing we have to deal with. If we compare our English words *farmer* and *goodness* with such words as *height* and *depth*, we cannot fail to be struck by a notable difference in the affixing technique of the two sets. The *-er* and *-ness* are affixed quite mechanically to radical elements which are at the same time independent words (*farm, good*). They are in no sense independently significant elements, but they convey their meaning (agentive, abstract quality) with unfailing directness. Their use is simple and regular and we should have no difficulty in appending them to any verb or to any adjective, however recent in origin. From a verb *to camouflage* we may form the noun *camouflager* "one who camouflages," from an adjective *jazzy* proceeds with perfect ease the noun *jazziness*. It is different with *height* and *depth*. Functionally they are related to *high* and *deep* precisely as is *goodness* to *good*, but the degree of coalescence between radical element and affix is greater. Radical element and affix, while measurably distinct, cannot be torn apart quite so readily as could the *good* and *-ness* of *goodness*. The *-t* of *height* is not the typical form of the affix (compare *strength, length, filth, breadth, youth*), while *dep-* is not identical with *deep*. We may designate the two types of affixing as "fusing" and "juxtaposing." The juxtaposing technique we may call an "agglutinative" one, if we like.

Is the fusing technique thereby set off as the essence of inflection? I am afraid that we have not yet reached our goal. If our language were crammed full of coalescences of the type of *depth*, but if, on the other hand, it used the plural independently of verb concord (e.g., *the books falls* like *the book falls*, or *the book fall* like *the books fall*), the personal endings independently of tense (e.g., *the book fells* like *the book falls*, or *the book fall* like *the book fell*), and the pronouns independently of case (e.g., *I see he* like *he sees me*, or *him see the man* like *the man sees him*), we should hesitate to describe it as inflective. The mere fact of fusion does not seem to satisfy us as a clear indication of the inflective process. There are, indeed, a large number of languages that fuse radical element and affix in as complete and intricate a fashion as one could hope to find anywhere without thereby giving signs of that particular kind of formalism that marks off such languages as Latin and Greek as inflective.

What is true of fusion is equally true of the "symbolic" processes. [[105]] There are linguists that speak of alternations like *drink* and *drank* as though they represented the high-water mark of inflection, a kind of spiritualized essence of pure inflective form. In such Greek forms, nevertheless, as *pepomph-a* "I have sent," as contrasted with *pemp-o* "I send," with its trebly symbolic change of the radical element (reduplicating *pe-*, change of *e* to *o*, change of *p* to *ph*), it is rather the peculiar alternation of the first person singular *-a* of the perfect with the *-o* of the present that gives them their inflective cast. Nothing could be more erroneous than to imagine that symbolic changes of the radical element, even for the expression of such abstract concepts as those of number and tense, is always associated with the syntactic peculiarities of an inflective language. If by an "agglutinative" language we mean one that affixes according to the juxtaposing technique, then we can only say that there are hundreds of fusing and symbolic languages—non-agglutinative by definition—that are, for all that, quite alien in spirit to the inflective type of Latin and Greek. We can call such languages inflective, if we like, but we must then be prepared to revise radically our notion of inflective form.

It is necessary to understand that fusion of the radical element and the affix may be taken in a broader psychological sense than I have yet indicated. If every noun plural in English were of the type of *book*: *books*, if there were not such conflicting patterns as *deer*: *deer*, *ox*: *oxen*, *goose*: *geese* to complicate the general form picture of plurality, there is little doubt that the fusion of the elements *book* and *-s* into the unified word *books* would be felt as a little less complete than it actually is. One reasons, or feels, unconsciously about the matter somewhat as follows:—If the form pattern represented by the word *books* is identical, as far as use is concerned, with that of the word *oxen*, the pluralizing elements *-s* and *-en* cannot have quite so definite, quite so autonomous, a value as we might at first be inclined to suppose. They are plural elements only in so far as plurality is predicated of certain selected concepts. The words *books* and *oxen* are therefore a little other than mechanical combinations of the symbol of a thing (*book*, *ox*) and a clear symbol of plurality. There is a slight psychological uncertainty or haze about the juncture in *book-s* and *ox-en*. A little of the force of *-s* and *-en* is anticipated by, or appropriated by, the words *book* and *ox* themselves, just as the conceptual force of *-th* in *dep-th* is appreciably weaker than that of *-ness* in *good-ness* in spite of the functional parallelism between *depth* and *goodness*. Where there is uncertainty about the juncture, where the affixed element cannot rightly claim to possess its full share of significance, the unity of the complete word is more strongly emphasized. The mind must rest on something. If it cannot linger on the constituent elements, it hastens all the more eagerly to the acceptance of the word as a whole. A word like *goodness* illustrates "agglutination," *books* "regular fusion," *depth* "irregular fusion," *geese* "symbolic fusion" or "symbolism." [106]

The psychological distinctness of the affixed elements in an agglutinative term may be even more marked than in the *-ness* of *goodness*. To be strictly accurate, the significance of the *-ness* is not quite as inherently determined, as autonomous, as it might be. It is at the mercy of the preceding radical element to this extent, that it requires to be preceded by a particular type of such element, an adjective. Its own power is thus, in a manner, checked in advance. The fusion here, however, is so vague and elementary, so much a matter of course in the great majority of all cases of affixing, that it is natural to overlook its reality and to emphasize rather the juxtaposing or agglutinative nature of the affixing process. If the *-ness* could be affixed as an abstractive element to each and every type of radical element, if we could say *fightness* ("the act or quality of fighting") or *waterness* ("the quality or state of water") or *awayness* ("the state of being away") as we can say *goodness* ("the state of being good"), we should have moved appreciably nearer the agglutinative pole. A language that runs to synthesis of this loose-jointed sort may be looked upon as an example of the ideal agglutinative type, particularly if the concepts expressed by the agglutinated elements are relational or, at the least, belong to the abstracter class of derivational ideas.

Instructive forms may be cited from Nootka. We shall return to our "fire in the house." [107] The Nootka word *inikw-ihl* "fire in the house" is not as definitely formalized a word as its translation, suggests. The radical element *inikw-* "fire" is really as much of a verbal as of a nominal term; it may be rendered now by "fire," now by "burn," according to the syntactic exigencies of the sentence. The derivational element *-ihl* "in the house" does not mitigate this vagueness or generality; *inikw-ihl* is still "fire in the house" or "burn in the house." It may be definitely nominalized or verbalized by the affixing of elements that are exclusively nominal or verbal in force. For example, *inikw-ihl-'i*, with its suffixed article, is a clear-cut nominal form: "the burning in the house, the fire in the house"; *inikw-ihl-ma*, with its indicative suffix, is just as clearly verbal: "it burns in the house." How weak must be the degree of fusion between "fire in the house" and the nominalizing or verbalizing suffix is apparent from the fact that the formally indifferent *inikwihl* is not an abstraction gained by analysis but a full-fledged word, ready for use in the sentence. The nominalizing *-'i* and the indicative *-ma* are not fused form-affixes, they are simply additions of formal import. But we can continue to hold the verbal or nominal nature of *inikwihl* in abeyance long before we reach the *-'i* or *-ma*. We can pluralize it: *inikw-ihl-'minih*; it is still either "fires in the house" or "burn plurally in the house." We can diminutivize this plural: *inikw-ihl-'minih-'is*, "little fires in the house" or "burn plurally and slightly in the house." What if we add the preterit tense suffix *-it*? Is not *inikw-ihl-'minih-'is-it* necessarily a verb: "several small fires were burning in the house"? It is not. It may still be nominalized; *inikwihl'minih'isit-'i* means "the former small fires in the house, the little fires that were once burning in the house." It is not an unambiguous verb until it is given a form that excludes every other possibility, as in the indicative *inikwihl-minih'isit-a* "several small fires were burning in the house." We recognize at once that the elements *-ihl*, *-'minih*, *-'is*, and *-it*, quite aside from the relatively concrete or abstract nature of their content and aside, further, from the degree of their outer (phonetic) cohesion with the elements that precede them, have a psychological independence that our own affixes never have. They are typically agglutinated elements, though they have no greater external independence, are no more capable of living apart from the radical element to which they are suffixed, than the *-ness* and *goodness* or the *-s* of *books*. It does not follow that an agglutinative language may not make use of the principle of fusion, both external and psychological, or even of symbolism to a considerable extent. It is a question of tendency. Is the formative slant clearly towards the agglutinative method? Then the language is "agglutinative." As such, it may be prefixing or suffixing, analytic, synthetic, or polysynthetic.

To return to inflection. An inflective language like Latin or Greek uses the method of fusion, and this fusion has an inner psychological as well as an outer phonetic meaning. But it is not enough that the fusion operate merely in the sphere of derivational concepts (group II), [[108]] it must involve the syntactic relations, which may either be expressed in unalloyed form (group IV) or, as in Latin and Greek, as "concrete relational concepts" (group III). [[109]] As far as Latin and Greek are concerned, their inflection consists essentially of the fusing of elements that express logically impure relational concepts with radical elements and with elements expressing derivational concepts. Both fusion as a general method and the expression of relational concepts in the word are necessary to the notion of "inflection."

But to have thus defined inflection is to doubt the value of the term as descriptive of a major class. Why emphasize both a technique and a particular content at one and the same time? Surely we should be clear in our minds as to whether we set more store by one or the other. "Fusional" and "symbolic" contrast with "agglutinative," which is not on a par with "inflective" at all. What are we to do with the fusional and symbolic languages that do not express relational concepts in the word but leave them to the sentence? And are we not to distinguish between agglutinative languages that express these same concepts in the word—in so far inflective-like—and those that do not? We dismissed the scale: analytic, synthetic, polysynthetic, as too merely quantitative for our purpose. Isolating, affixing, symbolic—this also seemed insufficient for the reason that it laid too much stress on technical externals. Isolating, agglutinative, fusional, and symbolic is a preferable scheme, but still skirts the external. We shall do best, it seems to me, to hold to "inflective" as a valuable suggestion for a broader and more consistently developed scheme, as a hint for a classification based on the nature of the concepts expressed by the language. The other two classifications, the first based on degree of synthesis, the second on degree of fusion, may be retained as intercrossing schemes that give us the opportunity to subdivide our main conceptual types.

It is well to recall that all languages must needs express radical concepts (group I) and relational ideas (group IV). Of the two other large groups of concepts—derivational (group II) and mixed relational (group III)—both may be absent, both present, or only one present. This gives us at once a simple, incisive, and absolutely inclusive method of classifying all known languages. They are:

A. Such as express only concepts of groups I and IV; in other words, languages that keep the syntactic relations pure and that do not possess the power to modify the significance of their radical elements by means of affixes or internal changes.[110] We may call these *Pure-relational non-deriving languages* or, more tersely, *Simple Pure-relational languages*. These are the languages that cut most to the bone of linguistic expression.
B. Such as express concepts of groups I, II, and IV; in other words, languages that keep the syntactic relations pure and that also possess the power to modify the significance of their radical elements by means of affixes or internal changes. These are the *Pure-relational deriving languages* or *Complex Pure-relational languages*.
C. Such as express concepts of groups I and III;[111] in other words, languages in which the syntactic relations are expressed in necessary connection with concepts that are not utterly devoid of concrete significance but that do not, apart from such mixture, possess the power to modify the significance of their radical elements by means of affixes or internal changes.[112] These are the *Mixed-relational non-deriving languages* or *Simple Mixed-relational languages*.
D. Such as express concepts of groups I, II, and III; in other words, languages in which the syntactic relations are expressed in mixed form, as in C, and that also possess the power to modify the significance of their radical elements by means of affixes or internal changes. These are the *Mixed-relational deriving languages* or *Complex Mixed-relational languages*. Here belong the "inflective" languages that we are most familiar with as well as a great many "agglutinative" languages, some "polysynthetic," others merely synthetic.

This conceptual classification of languages, I must repeat, does not attempt to take account of the technical externals of language. It answers, in effect, two fundamental questions concerning the translation of concepts into linguistic symbols. Does the language, in the first place, keep its radical concepts pure or does it build up its concrete ideas by an aggregation of inseparable elements (types A and C *versus* types B and D)? And, in the second place, does it keep the basic relational concepts, such as are absolutely unavoidable in the ordering of a proposition, free of an admixture of the concrete or not (types A and B *versus* types C and D)? The second question, it seems to me, is the more fundamental of the two. We can therefore simplify our classification and present it in the following form:

I. Pure-relational Languages { A. Simple
B. Complex

II. Mixed-relational Languages { C. Simple
D. Complex

The classification is too sweeping and too broad for an easy, descriptive survey of the many varieties of human speech. It needs to be amplified. Each of the types A, B, C, D may be subdivided into an agglutinative, a fusional, and a symbolic sub-type, according to the prevailing method of modification of the radical element. In type A we distinguish in addition an isolating sub-type, characterized by the absence of all affixes and modifications of the radical element. In the isolating languages the syntactic relations are expressed by the position of the words in the sentence. This is also true of many languages of type B, the terms "agglutinative," "fusional," and "symbolic" applying in their case merely to the treatment of the derivational, not the relational, concepts. Such languages could be termed "agglutinative-isolating," "fusional-isolating" and "symbolic-isolating."

This brings up the important general consideration that the method of handling one group of concepts need not in the least be identical with that used for another. Compound terms could be used to indicate this difference, if desired, the first element of the compound referring to the treatment of the concepts of group II, the second to that of the concepts of groups III and IV. An "agglutinative" language would normally be taken to mean one that agglutinates all of its affixed elements or that does so to a preponderating extent. In an "agglutinative-fusional" language the derivational elements are agglutinated, perhaps in the form of prefixes, while the relational elements (pure or mixed) are fused with the radical element, possibly as another set of prefixes following the first set or in the form of suffixes or as part prefixes and part suffixes. By a "fusional-agglutinative" language we would understand one that fuses its derivational elements but allows a greater independence to those that indicate relations. All these and similar distinctions are not merely theoretical possibilities, they can be abundantly illustrated from the descriptive facts of linguistic morphology. Further, should it prove desirable to insist on the degree of elaboration of the word, the terms "analytic," "synthetic," and "polysynthetic" can be added as descriptive terms. It goes without saying that languages of type A are necessarily analytic and that languages of type C also are prevailingly analytic and are not likely to develop beyond the synthetic stage.

But we must not make too much of terminology. Much depends on the relative emphasis laid on this or that feature or point of view. The method of classifying languages here developed has this great advantage, that it can be refined or simplified according to the needs of a particular discussion. The degree of synthesis may be entirely ignored; "fusion" and "symbolism" may often be combined with advantage under the head of "fusion"; even the difference between agglutination and fusion may, if desired, be set aside as either too difficult to draw or as irrelevant to the issue. Languages, after all, are exceedingly complex historical structures. It is of less importance to put each language in a neat pigeon-hole than to have evolved a flexible method which enables us to place it, from two or three independent standpoints, relatively to another language. All this is not to deny that certain linguistic types are more stable and frequently represented than others that are just as possible from a theoretical standpoint. But we are too ill-informed as yet of the structural spirit of great numbers of languages to have the right to frame a classification that is other than flexible and experimental.

The reader will gain a somewhat livelier idea of the possibilities of linguistic morphology by glancing down the subjoined analytical table of selected types. The columns II, III, IV refer to the groups of concepts so numbered in the preceding chapter. The letters *a, b, c, d* refer respectively to the processes of isolation (position in the sentence), agglutination, fusion, and symbolism. Where more than one technique is employed, they are put in the order of their importance. [113]

Fundamental Type	I	II	III	Technique	Synthesis	Examples
A (Simple Pure-relational)	—	—	a	Isolating	Analytic	Chinese; Annamite
	(d)	—	a, b	Isolating (weakly agglutinative)	Analytic	Ewe (Guinea Coast)

	(b)	—	a, b, c	Agglutinative (mildly agglutinative-fusional)	Analytic	Modern Tibetan
B (Complex Pure-relational)	b, (d)	—	a	Agglutinative-isolating	Analytic	Polynesian
	b	—	a, (b)	Agglutinative-isolating	Polysynthetic	Haida
	c	—	a	Fusional-isolating	Analytic	Cambodgian
	b	—	b	Agglutinative	Synthetic	Turkish
	b, d	(b)	b	Agglutinative (symbolic tinge)	Polysynthetic	Yana (N. California)
	c, d, (b)	—	a, b	Fusional-agglutinative (symbolic tinge)	Synthetic (mildly)	Classical Tibetan
	b	—	c	Agglutinative-fusional	Synthetic (mildly polysynthetic)	Sioux
	c	—	c	Fusional	Synthetic	Salinan (S.W. California)
	d, c	(d)	d, c, a	Symbolic	Analytic	Shilluk (Upper Nile)
C (Simple Mixed-relational)	(b)	b	—	Agglutinative	Synthetic	Bantu
	(c)	c, (d)	a	Fusional	Analytic (mildly synthetic)	French [114]
D (Complex Mixed-relational)	b, c, d	b	b	Agglutinative (symbolic tinge)	Polysynthetic	Nootka (Vancouver Island) [115]
	c, (d)	b	—	Fusional-agglutinative	Polysynthetic (mildly)	Chinook (lower

					Columbia R.)
c, (d)	c, (d), (b)	—	Fusional	Polysynthetic	Algonkin
c	c, d	a	Fusional	Analytic	English
c, d	c, d	—	Fusional (symbolic tinge)	Synthetic	Latin, Greek, Sanskrit
c, b, d	c, d	(a)	Fusional (strongly symbolic)	Synthetic	Takelma (S.W. Oregon)
d, c	c, d	(a)	Symbolic-fusional	Synthetic	Semitic (Arabic, Hebrew)

I need hardly point out that these examples are far from exhausting the possibilities of linguistic structure. Nor that the fact that two languages are similarly classified does not necessarily mean that they present a great similarity on the surface. We are here concerned with the most fundamental and generalized features of the spirit, the technique, and the degree of elaboration of a given language. Nevertheless, in numerous instances we may observe this highly suggestive and remarkable fact, that languages that fall into the same class have a way of paralleling each other in many details or in structural features not envisaged by the scheme of classification. Thus, a most interesting parallel could be drawn on structural lines between Takelma and Greek, [[116]] languages that are as geographically remote from each other and as unconnected in a historical sense as two languages selected at random can well be. Their similarity goes beyond the generalized facts registered in the table. It would almost seem that linguistic features that are easily thinkable apart from each other, that seem to have no necessary connection in theory, have nevertheless a tendency to cluster or to follow together in the wake of some deep, controlling impulse to form that dominates their drift. If, therefore, we can only be sure of the intuitive similarity of two given languages, of their possession of the same submerged form-feeling, we need not be too much surprised to find that they seek and avoid certain linguistic developments in common. We are at present very far from able to define just what these fundamental form intuitions are. We can only feel them rather vaguely at best and must content ourselves for the most part with noting their symptoms. These symptoms are being garnered in our descriptive and historical grammars of diverse languages. Some day, it may be, we shall be able to read from them the great underlying ground-plans.

Such a purely technical classification of languages as the current one into "isolating," "agglutinative," and "inflective" (read "fusional") cannot claim to have great value as an entering wedge into the discovery of the intuitional forms of language. I do not know whether the suggested classification into four conceptual groups is likely to drive deeper or not. My own feeling is that it does, but classifications, neat constructions of the speculative mind, are slippery things. They have to be tested at every possible opportunity before they have the right to cry for acceptance. Meanwhile we may take some encouragement from the application of a rather curious, yet simple, historical test. Languages are in constant process of change, but it is only reasonable to suppose that they tend to preserve longest what is most fundamental in their structure. Now if we take great groups of genetically related languages,[117] we find that as we pass from one to another or trace the course of their development we frequently encounter a gradual change of morphological type. This is not surprising, for there is no reason why a language should remain permanently true to its original form. It is interesting, however, to note that of the three intercrossing classifications represented in our table (conceptual type, technique, and degree of synthesis), it is the degree of synthesis that seems to change most readily, that the technique is modifiable but far less readily so, and that the conceptual type tends to persist the longest of all.

The illustrative material gathered in the table is far too scanty to serve as a real basis of proof, but it is highly suggestive as far as it goes. The only changes of conceptual type within groups of related languages that are to be gleaned from the table are of B to A (Shilluk as contrasted with Ewe;[118] Classical Tibetan as contrasted with Modern Tibetan and Chinese) and of D to C (French as contrasted with Latin[119]). But types A : B and C : D are respectively related to each other as a simple and a complex form of a still more fundamental type (pure-relational, mixed-relational). Of a passage from a pure-relational to a mixed-relational type or *vice versa* I can give no convincing examples.

The table shows clearly enough how little relative permanence there is in the technical features of language. That highly synthetic languages (Latin; Sanskrit) have frequently broken down into analytic forms (French; Bengali) or that agglutinative languages (Finnish) have in many instances gradually taken on "inflective" features are well-known facts, but the natural inference does not seem to have been often drawn that possibly the contrast between synthetic and analytic or agglutinative and "inflective" (fusional) is not so fundamental after all. Turning to the Indo-Chinese languages, we find that Chinese is as near to being a perfectly isolating language as any example we are likely to find, while Classical Tibetan has not only fusional but strong symbolic features (e.g., *g-tong-ba* "to give," past *b-tang*, future *gtang*, imperative *thong*); but both are pure-relational languages. Ewe is either isolating or only barely agglutinative, while Shilluk, though soberly analytic, is one of the most definitely symbolic languages I know; both of these Soudanese languages are pure-relational. The relationship between Polynesian and Cambodgian is remote, though practically certain; while the latter has more markedly fusional features than the former,[120] both conform to the complex pure-relational type. Yana and Salinan are superficially very dissimilar languages. Yana is highly polysynthetic and quite typically agglutinative, Salinan is no more synthetic than and as irregularly and compactly fusional ("inflective") as Latin; both are pure-relational, Chinook and Takelma, remotely related languages of Oregon, have diverged very far from each other, not only as regards technique and synthesis in general but in almost all the details of their structure; both are complex mixed-relational languages, though in very different ways. Facts such as these seem to lend color to the suspicion that in the contrast of pure-relational and mixed-relational (or concrete-relational) we are confronted by something deeper, more far-reaching, than the contrast of isolating, agglutinative, and fusional.[121]

Language as a Historical Product: Drift

Every one knows that language is variable. Two individuals of the same generation and locality, speaking precisely the same dialect and moving in the same social circles, are never absolutely at one in their speech habits. A minute investigation of the speech of each individual would reveal countless differences of detail—in choice of words, in sentence structure, in the relative frequency with which particular forms or combinations of words are used, in the pronunciation of particular vowels and consonants and of combinations of vowels and consonants, in all those features, such as speed, stress, and tone, that give life to spoken language. In a sense they speak slightly divergent dialects of the same language rather than identically the same language.

There is an important difference, however, between individual and dialectic variations. If we take two closely related dialects, say English as spoken by the "middle classes" of London and English as spoken by the average New Yorker, we observe that, however much the individual speakers in each city differ from each other, the body of Londoners forms a compact, relatively unified group in contrast to the body of New Yorkers. The individual variations are swamped in or absorbed by certain major agreements—say of pronunciation and vocabulary—which stand out very strongly when the language of the group as a whole is contrasted with that of the other group. This means that there is something like an ideal linguistic entity dominating the speech habits of the members of each group, that the sense of almost unlimited freedom which each individual feels in the use of his language is held in leash by a tacitly directing norm. One individual plays on the norm in a way peculiar to himself, the next individual is nearer the dead average in that particular respect in which the first speaker most characteristically departs from it but in turn diverges from the average in a way peculiar to himself, and so on. What keeps the individual's variations from rising to dialectic importance is not merely the fact that they are in any event of small moment—there are well-marked dialectic variations that are of no greater magnitude than individual variations within a dialect—it is chiefly that they are silently "corrected" or canceled by the consensus of usage. If all the speakers of a given dialect were arranged in order in accordance with the degree of their conformity to average usage, there is little doubt that they would constitute a very finely intergrading series clustered about a well-defined center or norm. The differences between any two neighboring speakers of the series [[122]] would be negligible for any but the most microscopic linguistic research. The differences between the outer-most members of the series are sure to be considerable, in all likelihood considerable enough to measure up to a true dialectic variation. What prevents us from saying that these untypical individuals speak distinct dialects is that their peculiarities, as a unified whole, are not referable to another norm than the norm of their own series.

If the speech of any member of the series could actually be made to fit into another dialect series, [[123]] we should have no true barriers between dialects (and languages) at all. We should merely have a continuous series of individual variations extending over the whole range of a historically unified linguistic area, and the cutting up of this large area (in some cases embracing parts of several continents) into distinct dialects and languages would be an essentially arbitrary proceeding with no warrant save that of practical convenience. But such a conception of the nature of dialectic variation does not correspond to the facts as we know them. Isolated individuals may be found who speak a compromise between two dialects of a language, and if their number and importance increases they may even end by creating a new dialectic norm of their own, a dialect in which the extreme peculiarities of the parent dialects are ironed out. In course of time the compromise dialect may absorb the parents, though more frequently these will tend to linger indefinitely as marginal forms of the enlarged dialect area. But such phenomena—and they are common enough in the history of language—are evidently quite secondary. They are closely linked with such social developments as the rise of nationality, the formation of literatures that aim to have more than a local appeal, the movement of rural populations into the cities, and all those other tendencies that break up the intense localism that unsophisticated man has always found natural.

The explanation of primary dialectic differences is still to seek. It is evidently not enough to say that if a dialect or language is spoken in two distinct localities or by two distinct social strata it naturally takes on distinctive forms, which in time come to be divergent enough to deserve the name of dialects. This is certainly true as far as it goes. Dialects do belong, in the first instance, to very definitely circumscribed social groups, homogeneous enough to secure the common feeling and purpose needed to create a norm. But the embarrassing question immediately arises, If all the individual variations within a dialect are being constantly leveled out to the dialectic norm, if there is no appreciable tendency for the individual's peculiarities to initiate a dialectic schism, why should we have dialectic variations at all? Ought not the norm, wherever and whenever threatened, automatically to reassert itself? Ought not the individual variations of each locality, even in the absence of intercourse between them, to cancel out to the same accepted speech average?

If individual variations "on a flat" were the only kind of variability in language, I believe we should be at a loss to explain why and how dialects arise, why it is that a linguistic prototype gradually breaks up into a number of mutually unintelligible languages. But language is not merely something that is spread out in space, as it were—a series of reflections in individual minds of one and the same timeless picture. Language moves down time in a current of its own making. It has a drift. If there were no breaking up of a language into dialects, if each language continued as a firm, self-contained unity, it would still be constantly moving away from any assignable norm, developing new features unceasingly and gradually transforming itself into a language so different from its starting point as to be in effect a new language. Now dialects arise not because of the mere fact of individual variation but because two or more groups of individuals have become sufficiently disconnected to drift apart, or independently, instead of together. So long as they keep strictly together, no amount of individual variation would lead to the formation of dialects. In practice, of course, no language can be spread over a vast territory or even over a considerable area without showing dialectic variations, for it is impossible to keep a large population from segregating itself into local groups, the language of each of which tends to drift independently. Under cultural conditions such as apparently prevail to-day, conditions that fight localism at every turn, the tendency to dialectic cleavage is being constantly counteracted and in part "corrected" by the uniformizing factors already referred to. Yet even in so young a country as America the dialectic differences are not inconsiderable.

Under primitive conditions the political groups are small, the tendency to localism exceedingly strong. It is natural, therefore, that the languages of primitive folk or of non-urban populations in general are differentiated into a great number of dialects. There are parts of the globe where almost every village has its own dialect. The life of the geographically limited community is narrow and intense; its speech is correspondingly peculiar to itself. It is exceedingly doubtful if a language will ever be spoken over a wide area without multiplying itself dialectically. No sooner are the old dialects ironed out by compromises or ousted by the spread and influence of the one dialect which is culturally predominant when a new crop of dialects arises to undo the leveling work of the past. This is precisely what happened in Greece, for instance. In classical antiquity there were spoken a large number of local dialects, several of which are represented in the literature. As the cultural supremacy of Athens grew, its dialect, the Attic, spread at the expense of the rest, until, in the so-called Hellenistic period following the Macedonian conquest, the Attic dialect, in the vulgarized form known as the "Koine," became the standard speech of all Greece. But this linguistic uniformity [[124]] did not long continue. During the two millennia that separate the Greek of to-day from its classical prototype the Koine gradually split up into a number of dialects. Now Greece is as richly diversified in speech as in the time of Homer, though the present local dialects, aside from those of Attica itself, are not the lineal descendants of the old dialects of pre-Alexandrian days. [[125]] The experience of Greece is not exceptional. Old dialects are being continually wiped out only to make room for new ones. Languages can change at so many points of phonetics, morphology, and vocabulary that it is not surprising that once the linguistic community is broken it should slip off in different directions. It would be too much to expect a locally diversified language to develop along strictly parallel lines. If once the speech of a locality has begun to drift on its own account, it is practically certain to move further and further away from its linguistic fellows. Failing the retarding effect of dialectic interinfluences, which I have already touched upon, a group of dialects is bound to diverge on the whole, each from all of the others.

In course of time each dialect itself splits up into sub-dialects, which gradually take on the dignity of dialects proper while the primary dialects develop into mutually unintelligible languages. And so the budding process continues, until the divergences become so great that none but a linguistic student, armed with his documentary evidence and with his comparative or reconstructive method, would infer that the languages in question were genealogically related, represented independent lines of development, in other words, from a remote and common starting point. Yet it is as certain as any historical fact can be that languages so little resembling each other as Modern Irish, English, Italian, Greek, Russian, Armenian, Persian, and Bengali are but end-points in the present of drifts that converge to a meeting-point in the dim past. There is naturally no reason to believe that this earliest "Indo-European" (or "Aryan") prototype which we can in part reconstruct, in part but dimly guess at, is itself other than a single "dialect" of a group that has either become largely extinct or is now further represented by languages too divergent for us, with our limited means, to recognize as clear kin. [126]

All languages that are known to be genetically related, i.e., to be divergent forms of a single prototype, may be considered as constituting a "linguistic stock." There is nothing final about a linguistic stock. When we set it up, we merely say, in effect, that thus far we can go and no farther. At any point in the progress of our researches an unexpected ray of light may reveal the "stock" as but a "dialect" of a larger group. The terms dialect, language, branch, stock—it goes without saying—are purely relative terms. They are convertible as our perspective widens or contracts. [127] It would be vain to speculate as to whether or not we shall ever be able to demonstrate that all languages stem from a common source. Of late years linguists have been able to make larger historical syntheses than were at one time deemed feasible, just as students of culture have been able to show historical connections between culture areas or institutions that were at one time believed to be totally isolated from each other. The human world is contracting not only prospectively but to the backward-probing eye of culture-history. Nevertheless we are as yet far from able to reduce the riot of spoken languages to a small number of "stocks." We must still operate with a quite considerable number of these stocks. Some of them, like Indo-European or Indo-Chinese, are spoken over tremendous reaches; others, like Basque, [128] have a curiously restricted range and are in all likelihood but dwindling remnants of groups that were at one time more widely distributed. As for the single or multiple origin of speech, it is likely enough that language as a human institution (or, if one prefers, as a human "faculty") developed but once in the history of the race, that all the complex history of language is a unique cultural event. Such a theory constructed "on general principles" is of no real interest, however, to linguistic science.

What lies beyond the demonstrable must be left to the philosopher or the romancer.

We must return to the conception of "drift" in language. If the historical changes that take place in a language, if the vast accumulation of minute modifications which in time results in the complete remodeling of the language, are not in essence identical with the individual variations that we note on every hand about us, if these variations are born only to die without a trace, while the equally minute, or even minuter, changes that make up the drift are forever imprinted on the history of the language, are we not imputing to this history a certain mystical quality? Are we not giving language a power to change of its own accord over and above the involuntary tendency of individuals to vary the norm? And if this drift of language is not merely the familiar set of individual variations seen in vertical perspective, that is historically, instead of horizontally, that is in daily experience, what is it? Language exists only in so far as it is actually used—spoken and heard, written and read. What significant changes take place in it must exist, to begin with, as individual variations. This is perfectly true, and yet it by no means follows that the general drift of language can be understood [129] from an exhaustive descriptive study of these variations alone. They themselves are random phenomena, [130] like the waves of the sea, moving backward and forward in purposeless flux. The linguistic drift has direction. In other words, only those individual variations embody it or carry it which move in a certain direction, just as only certain wave movements in the bay outline the tide. The drift of a language is constituted by the unconscious selection on the part of its speakers of those individual variations that are cumulative in some special direction. This direction may be inferred, in the main, from the past history of the language. In the long run any new feature of the drift becomes part and parcel of the common, accepted speech, but for a long time it may exist as a mere tendency in the speech of a few, perhaps of a despised few. As we look about us and observe current usage, it is not likely to occur to us that our language has a "slope," that the changes of the next few centuries are in a sense prefigured in certain obscure tendencies of the present and that these changes, when consummated, will be seen to be but continuations of changes that have been already effected. We feel rather that our language is practically a fixed system and that what slight changes are destined to take place in it are as likely to move in one direction as another. The feeling is fallacious. Our very uncertainty as to the impending details of change makes the eventual consistency of their direction all the more impressive.

Sometimes we can feel where the drift is taking us even while we struggle against it. Probably the majority of those who read these words feel that it is quite "incorrect" to say "Who did you see?" We readers of many books are still very careful to say "Whom did you see?" but we feel a little uncomfortable (uncomfortably proud, it may be) in the process. We are likely to avoid the locution altogether and to say "Who was it you saw?" conserving literary tradition (the "whom") with the dignity of silence.[131] The folk makes no apology. "Whom did you see?" might do for an epitaph, but "Who did you see?" is the natural form for an eager inquiry. It is of course the uncontrolled speech of the folk to which we must look for advance information as to the general linguistic movement. It is safe to prophesy that within a couple of hundred years from to-day not even the most learned jurist will be saying "Whom did you see?" By that time the "whom" will be as delightfully archaic as the Elizabethan "his" for "its."[132] No logical or historical argument will avail to save this hapless "whom." The demonstration "I: me = he: him = who: whom" will be convincing in theory and will go unheeded in practice.

Even now we may go so far as to say that the majority of us are secretly wishing they could say "Who did you see?" It would be a weight off their unconscious minds if some divine authority, overruling the lifted finger of the pedagogue, gave them *carte blanche*. But we cannot too frankly anticipate the drift and maintain caste. We must affect ignorance of whither we are going and rest content with our mental conflict— uncomfortable conscious acceptance of the "whom," unconscious desire for the "who."[133] Meanwhile we indulge our sneaking desire for the forbidden locution by the use of the "who" in certain twilight cases in which we can cover up our fault by a bit of unconscious special pleading. Imagine that some one drops the remark when you are not listening attentively, "John Smith is coming to-night." You have not caught the name and ask, not "Whom did you say?" but "Who did you say?" There is likely to be a little hesitation in the choice of the form, but the precedent of usages like "Whom did you see?" will probably not seem quite strong enough to induce a "Whom did you say?" Not quite relevant enough, the grammarian may remark, for a sentence like "Who did you say?" is not strictly analogous to "Whom did you see?" or "Whom did you mean?" It is rather an abbreviated form of some such sentence as "Who, did you say, is coming to-night?" This is the special pleading that I have referred to, and it has a certain logic on its side. Yet the case is more hollow than the grammarian thinks it to be, for in reply to such a query as "You're a good hand at bridge, John, aren't you?" John, a little taken aback, might mutter "Did you say me?" hardly "Did you say I?" Yet the logic for the latter ("Did you say I was a good hand at bridge?") is evident. The real point is that there is not enough vitality in the "whom" to carry it over such little difficulties as a "me" can compass without a thought. The proportion "I : me = he : him = who : whom" is logically and historically sound, but psychologically shaky. "Whom did you see?" is correct, but there is something false about its correctness.

It is worth looking into the reason for our curious reluctance to use locutions involving the word "whom" particularly in its interrogative sense. The only distinctively objective forms which we still possess in English are *me, him, her* (a little blurred because of its identity with the possessive *her*), *us, them,* and *whom*. In all other cases the objective has come to be identical with the subjective—that is, in outer form, for we are not now taking account of position in the sentence. We observe immediately in looking through the list of objective forms that *whom* is psychologically isolated. *Me, him, her, us,* and *them* form a solid, well-integrated group of objective personal pronouns parallel to the subjective series *I, he, she, we, they*. The forms *who* and *whom* are technically "pronouns" but they are not felt to be in the same box as the personal pronouns. *Whom* has clearly a weak position, an exposed flank, for words of a feather tend to flock together, and if one strays behind, it is likely to incur danger of life. Now the other interrogative and relative pronouns (*which, what, that*), with which *whom* should properly flock, do not distinguish the subjective and objective forms. It is psychologically unsound to draw the line of form cleavage between *whom* and the personal pronouns on the one side, the remaining interrogative and relative pronouns on the other. The form groups should be symmetrically related to, if not identical with, the function groups. Had *which, what,* and *that* objective forms parallel to *whom*, the position of this last would be more secure. As it is, there is something unesthetic about the word. It suggests a form pattern which is not filled out by its fellows. The only way to remedy the irregularity of form distribution is to abandon the *whom* altogether for we have lost the power to create new objective forms and cannot remodel our *which-what-that* group so as to make it parallel with the smaller group *who-whom*. Once this is done, *who* joins its flock and our unconscious desire for form symmetry is satisfied. We do not secretly chafe at "Whom did you see?" without reason. [[134]]

But the drift away from *whom* has still other determinants. The words *who* and *whom* in their interrogative sense are psychologically related not merely to the pronouns *which* and *what*, but to a group of interrogative adverbs—*where, when, how*—all of which are invariable and generally emphatic. I believe it is safe to infer that there is a rather strong feeling in English that the interrogative pronoun or adverb, typically an emphatic element in the sentence, should be invariable. The inflective *-m* of *whom* is felt as a drag upon the rhetorical effectiveness of the word. It needs to be eliminated if the interrogative pronoun is to receive all its latent power. There is still a third, and a very powerful, reason for the avoidance of *whom*. The contrast between the subjective and objective series of personal pronouns (*I, he, she, we, they*: *me, him, her, us, them*) is in English associated with a difference of position. We say *I see the man* but *the man sees me*; *he told him*, never *him he told* or *him told he*. Such usages as the last two are distinctly poetic and archaic; they are opposed to the present drift of the language. Even in the interrogative one does not say *Him did you see?* It is only in sentences of the type *Whom did you see?* that an inflected objective before the verb is now used at all. On the other hand, the order in *Whom did you see?* is imperative because of its interrogative form; the interrogative pronoun or adverb normally comes first in the sentence (*What are you doing? When did he go? Where are you from?*). In the "whom" of *Whom did you see?* there is concealed, therefore, a conflict between the order proper to a sentence containing an inflected objective and the order natural to a sentence with an interrogative pronoun or adverb. The solution *Did you see whom?* or *You saw whom?* [[135]] is too contrary to the idiomatic drift of our language to receive acceptance. The more radical solution *Who did you see?* is the one the language is gradually making for.

These three conflicts—on the score of form grouping, of rhetorical emphasis, and of order—are supplemented by a fourth difficulty. The emphatic *whom*, with its heavy build (half-long vowel followed by labial consonant), should contrast with a lightly tripping syllable immediately following. In *whom did*, however, we have an involuntary retardation that makes the locution sound "clumsy." This clumsiness is a phonetic verdict, quite apart from the dissatisfaction due to the grammatical factors which we have analyzed. The same prosodic objection does not apply to such parallel locutions as *what did* and *when did*. The vowels of *what* and *when* are shorter and their final consonants melt easily into the following *d*, which is pronounced in the same tongue position as *t* and *n*. Our instinct for appropriate rhythms makes it as difficult for us to feel content with *whom did* as for a poet to use words like *dreamed* and *hummed* in a rapid line. Neither common feeling nor the poet's choice need be at all conscious. It may be that not all are equally sensitive to the rhythmic flow of speech, but it is probable that rhythm is an unconscious linguistic determinant even with those who set little store by its artistic use. In any event the poet's rhythms can only be a more sensitive and stylized application of rhythmic tendencies that are characteristic of the daily speech of his people.

We have discovered no less than four factors which enter into our subtle disinclination to say "Whom did you see?" The uneducated folk that says "Who did you see?" with no twinge of conscience has a more acute flair for the genuine drift of the language than its students. Naturally the four restraining factors do not operate independently. Their separate energies, if we may make bold to use a mechanical concept, are "canalized" into a single force. This force or minute embodiment of the general drift of the language is psychologically registered as a slight hesitation in using the word *whom*. The hesitation is likely to be quite unconscious, though it may be readily acknowledged when attention is called to it. The analysis is certain to be unconscious, or rather unknown, to the normal speaker.[[136]] How, then, can we be certain in such an analysis as we have undertaken that all of the assigned determinants are really operative and not merely some one of them? Certainly they are not equally powerful in all cases. Their values are variable, rising and falling according to the individual and the locution.[[137]] But that they really exist, each in its own right, may sometimes be tested by the method of elimination. If one or other of the factors is missing and we observe a slight diminution in the corresponding psychological reaction ("hesitation" in our case), we may conclude that the factor is in other uses genuinely positive. The second of our four factors applies only to the interrogative use of *whom*, the fourth factor applies with more force to the interrogative than to the relative. We can therefore understand why a sentence like *Is he the man whom you referred to?* though not as idiomatic as *Is he the man (that) you referred to?* (remember that it sins against counts one and three), is still not as difficult to reconcile with our innate feeling for English expression as *Whom did you see?* If we eliminate the fourth factor from the interrogative usage, [138] say in *Whom are you looking at?* where the vowel following *whom* relieves this word of its phonetic weight, we can observe, if I am not mistaken, a lesser reluctance to use the *whom*. *Who are you looking at?* might even sound slightly offensive to ears that welcome *Who did you see?*

We may set up a scale of "hesitation values" somewhat after this fashion:

Value 1: factors 1, 3. "The man whom I referred to."
Value 2: factors 1, 3, 4. "The man whom they referred to."
Value 3: factors 1, 2, 3. "Whom are you looking at?"
Value 4: factors 1, 2, 3, 4. "Whom did you see?"

We may venture to surmise that while *whom* will ultimately disappear from English speech, locutions of the type *Whom did you see?* will be obsolete when phrases like *The man whom I referred to* are still in lingering use. It is impossible to be certain, however, for we can never tell if we have isolated all the determinants of a drift. In our particular case we have ignored what may well prove to be a controlling factor in the history of *who* and *whom* in the relative sense. This is the unconscious desire to leave these words to their interrogative function and to concentrate on *that* or mere word order as expressions of the relative (e.g., *The man that I referred to* or *The man I referred to*). This drift, which does not directly concern the use of *whom* as such (merely of *whom* as a form of *who*), may have made the relative *who* obsolete before the other factors affecting relative *whom* have run their course. A consideration like this is instructive because it indicates that knowledge of the general drift of a language is insufficient to enable us to see clearly what the drift is heading for. We need to know something of the relative potencies and speeds of the components of the drift.

It is hardly necessary to say that the particular drifts involved in the use of *whom* are of interest to us not for their own sake but as symptoms of larger tendencies at work in the language. At least three drifts of major importance are discernible. Each of these has operated for centuries, each is at work in other parts of our linguistic mechanism, each is almost certain to continue for centuries, possibly millennia. The first is the familiar tendency to level the distinction between the subjective and the objective, itself but a late chapter in the steady reduction of the old Indo-European system of syntactic cases. This system, which is at present best preserved in Lithuanian, [139] was already considerably reduced in the old Germanic language of which English, Dutch, German, Danish, and Swedish are modern dialectic forms. The seven Indo-European cases (nominative genitive, dative, accusative, ablative, locative, instrumental) had been already reduced to four (nominative genitive, dative, accusative). We know this from a careful comparison of and reconstruction based on the oldest Germanic dialects of which we still have records (Gothic, Old Icelandic, Old High German, Anglo-Saxon). In the group of West Germanic dialects, for the study of which Old High German, Anglo-Saxon, Old Frisian, and Old Saxon are our oldest and most valuable sources, we still have these four cases, but the phonetic form of the case syllables is already greatly reduced and in certain paradigms particular cases have coalesced. The case system is practically intact but it is evidently moving towards further disintegration. Within the Anglo-Saxon and early Middle English period there took place further changes in the same direction. The phonetic form of the case syllables became still further reduced and the distinction between the accusative and the dative finally disappeared. The new "objective" is really an amalgam of old accusative and dative forms; thus, *him*, the old dative (we still say *I give him the book*, not "abbreviated" from *I give to him*; compare Gothic *imma*, modern German *ihm*), took over the functions of the old accusative (Anglo-Saxon *hine*; compare Gothic *ina*, Modern German *ihn*) and dative. The distinction between the nominative and accusative was nibbled away by phonetic processes and morphological levelings until only certain pronouns retained distinctive subjective and objective forms.

In later medieval and in modern times there have been comparatively few apparent changes in our case system apart from the gradual replacement of *thou—thee* (singular) and subjective *ye*—objective *you* (plural) by a single undifferentiated form *you*. All the while, however, the case system, such as it is (subjective-objective, really absolutive, and possessive in nouns; subjective, objective, and possessive in certain pronouns) has been steadily weakening in psychological respects. At present it is more seriously undermined than most of us realize. The possessive has little vitality except in the pronoun and in animate nouns. Theoretically we can still say *the moon's phases* or *a newspaper's vogue*;

practically we limit ourselves pretty much to analytic locutions like *the phases of the moon* and *the vogue of a newspaper*. The drift is clearly toward the limitation, of possessive forms to animate nouns. All the possessive pronominal forms except *its* and, in part, *their* and *theirs*, are also animate. It is significant that *theirs* is hardly ever used in reference to inanimate nouns, that there is some reluctance to so use *their*, and that *its* also is beginning to give way to *of it*. *The appearance of it* or *the looks of it* is more in the current of the language than *its appearance*. It is curiously significant that *its young* (referring to an animal's cubs) is idiomatically preferable to *the young of it*. The form is only ostensibly neuter, in feeling it is animate; psychologically it belongs with *his children*, not with *the pieces of it*. Can it be that so common a word as *its* is actually beginning to be difficult? Is it too doomed to disappear? It would be rash to say that it shows signs of approaching obsolescence, but that it is steadily weakening is fairly clear.[140] In any event, it is not too much to say that there is a strong drift towards the restriction of the inflected possessive forms to animate nouns and pronouns.

How is it with the alternation of subjective and objective in the pronoun? Granted that *whom* is a weak sister, that the two cases have been leveled in *you* (in *it*, *that*, and *what* they were never distinct, so far as we can tell[141]), and that *her* as an objective is a trifle weak because of its formal identity with the possessive *her*, is there any reason to doubt the vitality of such alternations as *I see the man* and *the man sees me*? Surely the distinction between subjective *I* and objective *me*, between subjective *he* and objective *him*, and correspondingly for other personal pronouns, belongs to the very core of the language. We can throw *whom* to the dogs, somehow make shift to do without an *its*, but to level *I* and *me* to a single case—would that not be to un-English our language beyond recognition? There is no drift toward such horrors as *Me see him* or *I see he*. True, the phonetic disparity between *I* and *me*, *he* and *him*, *we* and *us*, has been too great for any serious possibility of form leveling. It does not follow that the case distinction as such is still vital. One of the most insidious peculiarities of a linguistic drift is that where it cannot destroy what lies in its way it renders it innocuous by washing the old significance out of it. It turns its very enemies to its own uses. This brings us to the second of the major drifts, the tendency to fixed position in the sentence, determined by the syntactic relation of the word.

We need not go into the history of this all-important drift. It is enough to know that as the inflected forms of English became scantier, as the syntactic relations were more and more inadequately expressed by the forms of the words themselves, position in the sentence gradually took over functions originally foreign to it. *The man* in *the man sees the dog* is subjective; in *the dog sees the man*, objective. Strictly parallel to these sentences are *he sees the dog* and *the dog sees him*. Are the subjective value of *he* and the objective value of *him* entirely, or even mainly, dependent on the difference of form? I doubt it. We could hold to such a view if it were possible to say *the dog sees he* or *him sees the dog*. It was once possible to say such things, but we have lost the power. In other words, at least part of the case feeling in *he* and *him* is to be credited to their position before or after the verb. May it not be, then, that *he* and *him*, *we* and *us*, are not so much subjective and objective forms as pre-verbal and post-verbal forms, very much as *my* and *mine* are now pre-nominal and post-nominal forms of the possessive (*my father* but *father mine*; *it is my book* but *the book is mine*)? That this interpretation corresponds to the actual drift of the English language is again indicated by the language of the folk. The folk says *it is me*, not *it is I*, which is "correct" but just as falsely so as the *whom did you see?* that we have analyzed. *I'm the one, it's me; we're the ones, it's us that will win out*—such are the live parallelisms in English to-day. There is little doubt that *it is I* will one day be as impossible in English as *c'est je*, for *c'est moi*, is now in French.

How differently our *I: me* feels than in Chaucer's day is shown by the Chaucerian *it am I*. Here the distinctively subjective aspect of the *I* was enough to influence the form of the preceding verb in spite of the introductory *it*; Chaucer's locution clearly felt more like a Latin *sum ego* than a modern *it is I* or colloquial *it is me*. We have a curious bit of further evidence to prove that the English personal pronouns have lost some share of their original syntactic force. Were *he* and *she* subjective forms pure and simple, were they not striving, so to speak, to become caseless absolutives, like *man* or any other noun, we should not have been able to coin such compounds as *he-goat* and *she-goat*, words that are psychologically analogous to *bull-moose* and *mother-bear*. Again, in inquiring about a new-born baby, we ask *Is it a he or a she?* quite as though *he* and *she* were the equivalents of *male* and *female* or *boy* and *girl*. All in all, we may conclude that our English case system is weaker than it looks and that, in one way or another, it is destined to get itself reduced to an absolutive (caseless) form for all nouns and pronouns but those that are animate. Animate nouns and pronouns are sure to have distinctive possessive forms for an indefinitely long period.

Meanwhile observe that the old alignment of case forms is being invaded by two new categories—a positional category (pre-verbal, post-verbal) and a classificatory category (animate, inanimate). The facts that in the possessive animate nouns and pronouns are destined to be more and more sharply distinguished from inanimate nouns and pronouns (*the man's*, but *of the house*; *his*, but *of it*) and that, on the whole, it is only animate pronouns that distinguish pre-verbal and post-verbal forms [143] are of the greatest theoretical interest. They show that, however the language strive for a more and more analytic form, it is by no means manifesting a drift toward the expression of "pure" relational concepts in the Indo-Chinese manner. [144] The insistence on the concreteness of the relational concepts is clearly stronger than the destructive power of the most sweeping and persistent drifts that we know of in the history and prehistory of our language.

The drift toward the abolition of most case distinctions and the correlative drift toward position as an all-important grammatical method are accompanied, in a sense dominated, by the last of the three major drifts that I have referred to. This is the drift toward the invariable word. In analyzing the "whom" sentence I pointed out that the rhetorical emphasis natural to an interrogative pronoun lost something by its form variability (*who, whose, whom*). This striving for a simple, unnuanced correspondence between idea and word, as invariable as may be, is very strong in English. It accounts for a number of tendencies which at first sight seem unconnected. Certain well-established forms, like the present third person singular *-s* of *works* or the plural *-s* of *books*, have resisted the drift to invariable words, possibly because they symbolize certain stronger form cravings that we do not yet fully understand. It is interesting to note that derivations that get away sufficiently from the concrete notion of the radical word to exist as independent conceptual centers are not affected by this elusive drift. As soon as the derivation runs danger of being felt as a mere nuancing of, a finicky play on, the primary concept, it tends to be absorbed by the radical word, to disappear as such. English words crave spaces between them, they do not like to huddle in clusters of slightly divergent centers of meaning, each edging a little away from the rest. *Goodness*, a noun of quality, almost a noun of relation, that takes its cue from the concrete idea of "good" without necessarily predicating that quality (e.g., *I do not think much of his goodness*) is sufficiently spaced from *good* itself not to need fear absorption. Similarly, *unable* can hold its own against *able* because it destroys the latter's sphere of influence; *unable* is psychologically as distinct from *able* as is *blundering* or *stupid*. It is different with adverbs in *-ly*. These lean too heavily on their adjectives to have the kind of vitality that English demands of its words. *Do it quickly!* drags psychologically. The nuance expressed by *quickly* is too close to that of *quick*, their circles of concreteness are too nearly the same, for the two words to feel comfortable together. The adverbs in *-ly* are likely to go to the wall in the not too distant future for this very reason and in face of their obvious usefulness. Another instance of the sacrifice of highly useful forms to this impatience of nuancing is the group *whence, whither, hence, hither, thence, thither*. They could not persist in live usage because they impinged too solidly upon the circles of meaning represented by the words *where, here* and *there*. In saying *whither* we feel too keenly that we repeat all of *where*. That we add to *where* an important nuance of direction irritates rather than satisfies. We prefer to merge the static and the directive (*Where do you live?* like *Where are you going?*) or, if need be, to overdo a little the concept of direction (*Where are you running to?*).

Now it is highly symptomatic of the nature of the drift away from word clusters that we do not object to nuances as such, we object to having the nuances formally earmarked for us. As a matter of fact our vocabulary is rich in near-synonyms and in groups of words that are psychologically near relatives, but these near-synonyms and these groups do not hang together by reason of etymology. We are satisfied with *believe* and *credible* just because they keep aloof from each other. *Good* and *well* go better together than *quick* and *quickly*. The English vocabulary is a rich medley because each English word wants its own castle. Has English long been peculiarly receptive to foreign words because it craves the staking out of as many word areas as possible, or, conversely, has the mechanical imposition of a flood of French and Latin loan-words, unrooted in our earlier tradition, so dulled our feeling for the possibilities of our native resources that we are allowing these to shrink by default? I suspect that both propositions are true. Each feeds on the other. I do not think it likely, however, that the borrowings in English have been as mechanical and external a process as they are generally represented to have been. There was something about the English drift as early as the period following the Norman Conquest that welcomed the new words. They were a compensation for something that was weakening within.

Language as a Historical Product: Phonetic Law

I have preferred to take up in some detail the analysis of our hesitation in using a locution like "Whom did you see?" and to point to some of the English drifts, particular and general, that are implied by this hesitation than to discuss linguistic change in the abstract. What is true of the particular idiom that we started with is true of everything else in language. Nothing is perfectly static. Every word, every grammatical element, every locution, every sound and accent is a slowly changing configuration, molded by the invisible and impersonal drift that is the life of language. The evidence is overwhelming that this drift has a certain consistent direction. Its speed varies enormously according to circumstances that it is not always easy to define. We have already seen that Lithuanian is to-day nearer its Indo-European prototype than was the hypothetical Germanic mother-tongue five hundred or a thousand years before Christ. German has moved more slowly than English; in some respects it stands roughly midway between English and Anglo-Saxon, in others it has of course diverged from the Anglo-Saxon line. When I pointed out in the preceding chapter that dialects formed because a language broken up into local segments could not move along the same drift in all of these segments, I meant of course that it could not move along identically the same drift. The general drift of a language has its depths. At the surface the current is relatively fast. In certain features dialects drift apart rapidly. By that very fact these features betray themselves as less fundamental to the genius of the language than the more slowly modifiable features in which the dialects keep together long after they have grown to be mutually alien forms of speech. But this is not all. The momentum of the more fundamental, the pre-dialectic, drift is often such that languages long disconnected will pass through the same or strikingly similar phases. In many such cases it is perfectly clear that there could have been no dialectic interinfluencing.

These parallelisms in drift may operate in the phonetic as well as in the morphological sphere, or they may affect both at the same time. Here is an interesting example. The English type of plural represented by *foot*: *feet*, *mouse*: *mice* is strictly parallel to the German *Fuss*: *Füsse*, *Maus*: *Mäuse*. One would be inclined to surmise that these dialectic forms go back to old Germanic or West-Germanic alternations of the same type. But the documentary evidence shows conclusively that there could have been no plurals of this type in primitive Germanic. There is no trace of such vocalic mutation ("umlaut") in Gothic, our most archaic Germanic language. More significant still is the fact that it does not appear in our oldest Old High German texts and begins to develop only at the very end of the Old High German period (circa 1000 A.D.). In the Middle High German period the mutation was carried through in all dialects. The typical Old High German forms are singular *fuoss*, plural *fuossi*; [[145]] singular *mus*, plural *musi*. The corresponding Middle High German forms are *fuoss*, *füesse*; *mus*, *müse*. Modern German *Fuss*: *Füsse*, *Maus*: *Mäuse* are the regular developments of these medieval forms. Turning to Anglo-Saxon, we find that our modern English forms correspond to *fot*, *fet*; *mus*, *mys*. [[146]] These forms are already in use in the earliest English monuments that we possess, dating from the eighth century, and thus antedate the Middle High German forms by three hundred years or more. In other words, on this particular point it took German at least three hundred years to catch up with a phonetic-morphological drift [[147]] that had long been under way in English. The mere fact that the affected vowels of related words (Old High German *uo*, Anglo-Saxon *o*) are not always the same shows that the affection took place at different periods in German and English. [[148]] There was evidently some general tendency or group of tendencies at work in early Germanic, long before English and German had developed as such, that eventually drove both of these dialects along closely parallel paths.

How did such strikingly individual alternations as *fot*: *fet*, *fuoss*: *füesse* develop? We have now reached what is probably the most central problem in linguistic history, gradual phonetic change. "Phonetic laws" make up a large and fundamental share of the subject-matter of linguistics. Their influence reaches far beyond the proper sphere of phonetics and invades that of morphology, as we shall see. A drift that begins as a slight phonetic readjustment or unsettlement may in the course of millennia bring about the most profound structural changes. The mere fact, for instance, that there is a growing tendency to throw the stress automatically on the first syllable of a word may eventually change the fundamental type of the language, reducing its final syllables to zero and driving it to the use of more and more analytical or symbolic [[149]] methods. The English phonetic laws involved in the rise of the words *foot*, *feet*, *mouse* and *mice* from their early West-Germanic prototypes *fot*, *foti*, *mus*, *musi* [[150]] may be briefly summarized as follows:

1. In *foti* "feet" the long *o* was colored by the following *i* to long *ö*, that is, *o* kept its lip-rounded quality and its middle height of tongue position but anticipated the front tongue position of the *i*; *ö* is the resulting compromise. This assimilatory change was regular, i.e., every accented long *o* followed by an *i* in the following syllable automatically developed to long *ö*; hence *tothi* "teeth" became *töthi*, *fodian* "to feed" became *födian*. At first there is no doubt the alternation between *o* and *ö* was not felt as intrinsically significant. It could only have been an unconscious mechanical adjustment such as may be observed in the speech of many to-day who modify the "oo" sound of words like *you* and *few* in the direction of German *ü* without, however, actually departing far enough from the "oo" vowel to prevent their acceptance of *who* and *you* as satisfactory rhyming words. Later on the quality of the *ö* vowel must have departed widely enough from that of *o* to enable *ö* to rise in consciousness [[151]] as a neatly distinct vowel. As soon as this happened, the expression of plurality in *föti*, *töthi*, and analogous words became symbolic and fusional, not merely fusional.
2. In *musi* "mice" the long *u* was colored by the following *i* to long *ü*. This change also was regular; *lusi* "lice" became *lüsi*, *kui* "cows" became *küi* (later simplified to *kü*; still preserved as *ki-* in *kine*), *fulian* "to make foul" became *fülian* (still preserved as *-file* in *defile*). The psychology of this phonetic law is entirely analogous to that of 1.
3. The old drift toward reducing final syllables, a rhythmic consequence of the strong Germanic stress on the first syllable, now manifested itself. The final *-i*, originally an important functional element, had long lost a great share of its value, transferred as that was to the symbolic vowel change (*o: ö*). It had little power of resistance, therefore, to the drift. It became dulled to a colorless *-e*; *föti* became *föte*.

4. The weak -*e* finally disappeared. Probably the forms *föte* and *föt* long coexisted as prosodic variants according to the rhythmic requirements of the sentence, very much as *Füsse* and *Füss'* now coexist in German.
5. The *ö* of *föt* became "unrounded" to long *e* (our present *a* of *fade*). The alternation of *fot: foti*, transitionally *fot: föti, föte, föt*, now appears as *fot: fet*. Analogously, *töth* appears as *teth*, *födian* as *fedian*, later *fedan*. The new long *e*-vowel "fell together" with the older *e*-vowel already existent (e.g., *her* "here," *he* "he"). Henceforward the two are merged and their later history is in common. Thus our present *he* has the same vowel as *feet*, *teeth*, and *feed*. In other words, the old sound pattern *o, e*, after an interim of *o, ö, e*, reappeared as *o, e*, except that now the *e* had greater "weight" than before.
6. *Fot: fet, mus: müs* (written *mys*) are the typical forms of Anglo-Saxon literature. At the very end of the Anglo-Saxon period, say about 1050 to 1100 A.D., the *ü*, whether long or short, became unrounded to *i*. *Mys* was then pronounced *mis* with long *i* (rhyming with present *niece*). The change is analogous to 5, but takes place several centuries later.
7. In Chaucer's day (circa 1350-1400 A.D.) the forms were still *fot: fet* (written *foot, feet*) and *mus: mis* (written very variably, but *mous, myse* are typical). About 1500 all the long *i*-vowels, whether original (as in *write, ride, wine*) or unrounded from Anglo-Saxon *ü* (as in *hide, bride, mice, defile*), became diphthongized to *ei* (i.e., *e* of *met* + short *i*). Shakespeare pronounced *mice* as *meis* (almost the same as the present Cockney pronunciation of *mace*).
8. About the same time the long *u*-vowels were diphthongized to *ou* (i.e., *o* of present Scotch *not* + *u* of *full*). The Chaucerian *mus: mis* now appears as the Shakespearean *mous: meis*. This change may have manifested itself somewhat later than 7; all English dialects have diphthongized old Germanic long *i*, but the long undiphthongized *u* is still preserved in Lowland Scotch, in which *house* and *mouse* rhyme with our *loose*. 7 and 8 are analogous developments, as were 5 and 6; 8 apparently lags behind 7 as 6, centuries earlier, lagged behind 7.
9. Some time before 1550 the long *e* of *fet* (written *feet*) took the position that had been vacated by the old long *i*, now diphthongized (see 7), i.e., *e* took the higher tongue position of *i*. Our (and Shakespeare's)

"long *e*" is, then, phonetically the same as the old long *i*. *Feet* now rhymed with the old *write* and the present *beat*.

10. About the same time the long *o* of *fot* (written *foot*) took the position that had been vacated by the old long *u*, now diphthongized (see 8), i.e., *o* took the higher tongue position of *u*. Our (and Shakespeare's) "long *oo*" is phonetically the same as the old long *u*. *Foot* now rhymed with the old *out* and the present *boot*. To summarize 7 to 10, Shakespeare pronounced *meis, mous, fit, fut*, of which *meis* and *mous* would affect our ears as a rather "mincing" rendering of our present *mice* and *mouse*, *fit* would sound practically identical with (but probably a bit more "drawled" than) our present *feet*, while *foot*, rhyming with *boot*, would now be set down as "broad Scotch."

11. Gradually the first vowel of the diphthong in *mice* (see 7) was retracted and lowered in position. The resulting diphthong now varies in different English dialects, but *ai* (i.e., *a* of *father*, but shorter, + short *i*) may be taken as a fairly accurate rendering of its average quality. [153] What we now call the "long *i*" (of words like *ride, bite, mice*) is, of course, an *ai*-diphthong. *Mice* is now pronounced *mais*.

12. Analogously to 11, the first vowel of the diphthong in *mouse* (see 8) was unrounded and lowered in position. The resulting diphthong may be phonetically rendered *au*, though it too varies considerably according to dialect. *Mouse*, then, is now pronounced *maus*.

13. The vowel of *foot* (see 10) became "open" in quality and shorter in quantity, i.e., it fell together with the old short *u*-vowel of words like *full, wolf, wool*. This change has taken place in a number of words with an originally long *u* (Chaucerian long close *o*), such as *forsook, hook, book, look, rook, shook*, all of which formerly had the vowel of *boot*. The older vowel, however, is still preserved in most words of this class, such as *fool, moon, spool, stoop*. It is highly significant of the nature of the slow spread of a "phonetic law" that there is local vacillation at present in several words. One hears *roof, soot*, and *hoop*, for instance, both with the "long" vowel of *boot* and the "short" of *foot*. It is impossible now, in other words, to state in a definitive manner what is the "phonetic law" that regulated the change of the older *foot* (rhyming with *boot*) to the present *foot*. We know that there is a strong drift towards the short, open vowel of *foot*, but whether or not all the old "long *oo*" words will eventually be affected we cannot

presume to say. If they all, or practically all, are taken by the drift, phonetic law 13 will be as "regular," as sweeping, as most of the twelve that have preceded it. If not, it may eventually be possible, if past experience is a safe guide, to show that the modified words form a natural phonetic group, that is, that the "law" will have operated under certain definable limiting conditions, e.g., that all words ending in a voiceless consonant (such as *p, t, k, f*) were affected (e.g., *hoof, foot, look, roof*), but that all words ending in the *oo*-vowel or in a voiced consonant remained unaffected (e.g., *do, food, move, fool*). Whatever the upshot, we may be reasonably certain that when the "phonetic law" has run its course, the distribution of "long" and "short" vowels in the old *oo*-words will not seem quite as erratic as at the present transitional moment. [[154]] We learn, incidentally, the fundamental fact that phonetic laws do not work with spontaneous automatism, that they are simply a formula for a consummated drift that sets in at a psychologically exposed point and gradually worms its way through a gamut of phonetically analogous forms.

It will be instructive to set down a table of form sequences, a kind of gross history of the words *foot, feet, mouse, mice* for the last 1500 years: [[155]]

I. *fot: foti; mus: musi* (West Germanic)
II. *fot: föti; mus: müsi*
III. *fot: föte; mus: müse*
IV. *fot: föt; mus: müs*
V. *fot: fet; mus: müs* (Anglo-Saxon)
VI. *fot: fet; mus: mis* (Chaucer)
VII. *fot: fet; mous: meis*
VIII. *fut* (rhymes with *boot*): *fit; mous: meis* (Shakespeare)
IX. *fut: fit; maus: mais*
X. *fut* (rhymes with *put*): *fit; maus: mais* (English of 1900)

It will not be necessary to list the phonetic laws that gradually differentiated the modern German equivalents of the original West Germanic forms from their English cognates. The following table gives a rough idea of the form sequences in German: [[156]]

I. *fot: foti; mus: musi* (West Germanic)
II. *foss: fossi; mus: musi*
III. *fuoss: fuossi; mus: musi* (Old High German)
IV. *fuoss: füessi; mus: müsi*
V. *fuoss: füesse; mus: müse* (Middle High German)
VI. *fuoss: füesse; mus: müze*
VII. *fuos: füese; mus: müze*
VIII. *fuos: füese; mous: möüze*
IX. *fus: füse; mous: möüze* (Luther)
X. *fus: füse; maus: moize* (German of 1900)

We cannot even begin to ferret out and discuss all the psychological problems that are concealed behind these bland tables. Their general parallelism is obvious. Indeed we might say that to-day the English and German forms resemble each other more than does either set the West Germanic prototypes from which each is independently derived. Each table illustrates the tendency to reduction of unaccented syllables, the vocalic modification of the radical element under the influence of the following vowel, the rise in tongue position of the long middle vowels (English *o* to *u*, *e* to *i*; German *o* to *uo* to *u*, *üe* to *ü*), the diphthongizing of the old high vowels (English *i* to *ei* to *ai*; English and German *u* to *ou* to *au*; German *ü* to *öü* to *oi*). These dialectic parallels cannot be accidental. They are rooted in a common, pre-dialectic drift.

Phonetic changes are "regular." All but one (English table, X.), and that as yet uncompleted, of the particular phonetic laws represented in our tables affect all examples of the sound in question or, if the phonetic change is conditional, all examples of the same sound that are analogously circumstanced. An example of the first type of change is the passage in English of all old long *i*-vowels to diphthongal *ai* via *ei*. The passage could hardly have been sudden or automatic, but it was rapid enough to prevent an irregularity of development due to cross drifts. The second type of change is illustrated in the development of Anglo-Saxon long *o* to long *e*, via *ö*, under the influence of a following *i*. In the first case we may say that *au* mechanically replaced long *u*, in the second that the old long *o* "split" into two sounds—long *o*, eventually *u*, and long *e*, eventually *i*. The former type of change did no violence to the old phonetic pattern, the formal distribution of sounds into groups; the latter type rearranged the pattern somewhat. If neither of the two sounds into which an old one "splits" is a new sound, it means that there has been a phonetic leveling, that two groups of words, each with a distinct sound or sound combination, have fallen together into one group. This kind of leveling is quite frequent in the history of language. In English, for instance, we have seen that all the old long *ü*-vowels, after they had become unrounded, were indistinguishable from the mass of long *i*-vowels. This meant that the long *i*-vowel became a more heavily weighted point of the phonetic pattern than before. It is curious to observe how often languages have striven to drive originally distinct sounds into certain favorite positions, regardless of resulting confusions. [160] In Modern Greek, for instance, the vowel *i* is the historical resultant of no less than ten etymologically distinct vowels (long and short) and diphthongs of the classical speech of Athens. There is, then, good evidence to show that there are general phonetic drifts toward particular sounds.

More often the phonetic drift is of a more general character. It is not so much a movement toward a particular set of sounds as toward particular types of articulation. The vowels tend to become higher or lower, the diphthongs tend to coalesce into monophthongs, the voiceless consonants tend to become voiced, stops tend to become spirants. As a matter of fact, practically all the phonetic laws enumerated in the two tables are but specific instances of such far-reaching phonetic drifts. The raising of English long *o* to *u* and of long *e* to *i*, for instance, was part of a general tendency to raise the position of the long vowels, just as the change of *t* to *ss* in Old High German was part of a general tendency to make voiceless spirants of the old voiceless stopped consonants. A single sound change, even if there is no phonetic leveling, generally threatens to upset the old phonetic pattern because it brings about a disharmony in the grouping of sounds. To reëstablish the old pattern without going back on the drift the only possible method is to have the other sounds of the series shift in analogous fashion. If, for some reason or other, *p* becomes shifted to its voiced correspondent *b*, the old series *p, t, k* appears in the unsymmetrical form *b, t, k*. Such a series is, in phonetic effect, not the equivalent of the old series, however it may answer to it in etymology. The general phonetic pattern is impaired to that extent. But if *t* and *k* are also shifted to their voiced correspondents *d* and *g*, the old series is reëstablished in a new form: *b, d, g*. The pattern as such is preserved, or restored. *Provided that* the new series *b, d, g* does not become confused with an old series *b, d, g* of distinct historical antecedents. If there is no such older series, the creation of a *b, d, g* series causes no difficulties. If there is, the old patterning of sounds can be kept intact only by shifting the old *b, d, g* sounds in some way. They may become aspirated to *bh, dh, gh* or spirantized or nasalized or they may develop any other peculiarity that keeps them intact as a series and serves to differentiate them from other series. And this sort of shifting about without loss of pattern, or with a minimum loss of it, is probably the most important tendency in the history of speech sounds. Phonetic leveling and "splitting" counteract it to some extent but, on the whole, it remains the central unconscious regulator of the course and speed of sound changes.

The desire to hold on to a pattern, the tendency to "correct" a disturbance by an elaborate chain of supplementary changes, often spread over centuries or even millennia—these psychic undercurrents of language are exceedingly difficult to understand in terms of individual psychology, though there can be no denial of their historical reality. What is the primary cause of the unsettling of a phonetic pattern and what is the cumulative force that selects these or those particular variations of the individual on which to float the pattern readjustments we hardly know. Many linguistic students have made the fatal error of thinking of sound change as a quasi-physiological instead of as a strictly psychological phenomenon, or they have tried to dispose of the problem by bandying such catchwords as "the tendency to increased ease of articulation" or "the cumulative result of faulty perception" (on the part of children, say, in learning to speak). These easy explanations will not do. "Ease of articulation" may enter in as a factor, but it is a rather subjective concept at best. Indians find hopelessly difficult sounds and sound combinations that are simple to us; one language encourages a phonetic drift that another does everything to fight. "Faulty perception" does not explain that impressive drift in speech sounds which I have insisted upon. It is much better to admit that we do not yet understand the primary cause or causes of the slow drift in phonetics, though we can frequently point to contributing factors. It is likely that we shall not advance seriously until we study the intuitional bases of speech. How can we understand the nature of the drift that frays and reforms phonetic patterns when we have never thought of studying sound patterning as such and the "weights" and psychic relations of the single elements (the individual sounds) in these patterns?

Every linguist knows that phonetic change is frequently followed by morphological rearrangements, but he is apt to assume that morphology exercises little or no influence on the course of phonetic history. I am inclined to believe that our present tendency to isolate phonetics and grammar as mutually irrelevant linguistic provinces is unfortunate. There are likely to be fundamental relations between them and their respective histories that we do not yet fully grasp. After all, if speech sounds exist merely because they are the symbolic carriers of significant concepts and groupings of concepts, why may not a strong drift or a permanent feature in the conceptual sphere exercise a furthering or retarding influence on the phonetic drift? I believe that such influences may be demonstrated and that they deserve far more careful study than they have received.

This brings us back to our unanswered question: How is it that both English and German developed the curious alternation of unmodified vowel in the singular (*foot, Fuss*) and modified vowel in the plural (*feet, Füsse*)? Was the pre-Anglo-Saxon alternation of *fot* and *fōti* an absolutely mechanical matter, without other than incidental morphological interest? It is always so represented, and, indeed, all the external facts support such a view. The change from *o* to *ö*, later *e*, is by no means peculiar to the plural. It is found also in the dative singular (*fet*), for it too goes back to an older *foti*. Moreover, *fet* of the plural applies only to the nominative and accusative; the genitive has *fota*, the dative *fotum*. Only centuries later was the alternation of *o* and *e* reinterpreted as a means of distinguishing number; *o* was generalized for the singular, *e* for the plural. Only when this reassortment of forms took place [[161]] was the modern symbolic value of the *foot: feet* alternation clearly established. Again, we must not forget that *o* was modified to *ö* (*e*) in all manner of other grammatical and derivative formations. Thus, a pre-Anglo-Saxon *hohan* (later *hon*) "to hang" corresponded to a *höhith, hehith* (later *hehth*) "hangs"; to *dom* "doom," *blod* "blood," and *fod* "food" corresponded the verbal derivatives *dömian* (later *deman*) "to deem," *blödian* (later *bledan*) "to bleed," and *födian* (later *fedan*) "to feed." All this seems to point to the purely mechanical nature of the modification of *o* to *ö* to *e*. So many unrelated functions were ultimately served by the vocalic change that we cannot believe that it was motivated by any one of them.

The German facts are entirely analogous. Only later in the history of the language was the vocalic alternation made significant for number. And yet consider the following facts. The change of *foti* to *fōti* antedated that of *fōti* to *fōte, fōt*. This may be looked upon as a "lucky accident," for if *foti* had become *fote, fot* before the *-i* had had the chance to exert a retroactive influence on the *o*, there would have been no difference between the singular and the plural. This would have been anomalous in Anglo-Saxon for a masculine noun. But was the sequence of phonetic changes an "accident"? Consider two further facts. All the Germanic languages were familiar with vocalic change as possessed of functional significance. Alternations like *sing, sang, sung* (Anglo-Saxon *singan, sang, sungen*) were ingrained in the linguistic consciousness. Further, the tendency toward the weakening of final syllables was very strong even then and had been manifesting itself in one way and another for centuries. I believe that these further facts help us to understand the actual sequence of phonetic changes. We may go so far as to say that the *o* (and *u*) could afford to stay the change to *ö* (and *ü*) until the destructive drift had advanced to the point where failure to modify the vowel would soon result in morphological embarrassment. At a certain moment the *-i* ending of the plural (and analogous endings with *i* in other formations) was felt to be too weak to quite bear its functional burden. The unconscious Anglo-Saxon mind, if I may be allowed a somewhat summary way of putting the complex facts, was glad of the opportunity afforded by certain individual variations, until then automatically canceled out, to have some share of the burden thrown on them. These particular variations won through because they so beautifully allowed the general phonetic drift to take its course without unsettling the morphological contours of the language. And the presence of symbolic variation (*sing, sang, sung*) acted as an attracting force on the rise of a new variation of similar character. All these factors were equally true of the German vocalic shift. Owing to the fact that the destructive phonetic drift was proceeding at a slower rate in German than in English, the preservative change of *uo* to *üe* (*u* to *ü*) did not need to set in until 300 years or more after the analogous English change. Nor did it. And this is to my mind a highly significant fact. Phonetic changes may sometimes be unconsciously encouraged in order to keep intact the psychological spaces between words and word forms. The general drift seizes upon those individual sound variations that help to preserve the morphological balance or to lead to the new balance that the language is striving for.

I would suggest, then, that phonetic change is compacted of at least three basic strands: (1) A general drift in one direction, concerning the nature of which we know almost nothing but which may be suspected to be of prevailingly dynamic character (tendencies, e.g., to greater or less stress, greater or less voicing of elements); (2) A readjusting tendency which aims to preserve or restore the fundamental phonetic pattern of the language; (3) A preservative tendency which sets in when a too serious morphological unsettlement is threatened by the main drift. I do not imagine for a moment that it is always possible to separate these strands or that this purely schematic statement does justice to the complex forces that guide the phonetic drift. The phonetic pattern of a language is not invariable, but it changes far less readily than the sounds that compose it. Every phonetic element that it possesses may change radically and yet the pattern remain unaffected. It would be absurd to claim that our present English pattern is identical with the old Indo-European one, yet it is impressive to note that even at this late day the English series of initial consonants:

p	t	k
b	d	g
f	th	h

corresponds point for point to the Sanskrit series:

b	d	g
bh	dh	gh
p	t	k

The relation between phonetic pattern and individual sound is roughly parallel to that which obtains between the morphologic type of a language and one of its specific morphological features. Both phonetic pattern and fundamental type are exceedingly conservative, all superficial appearances to the contrary notwithstanding. Which is more so we cannot say. I suspect that they hang together in a way that we cannot at present quite understand.

If all the phonetic changes brought about by the phonetic drift were allowed to stand, it is probable that most languages would present such irregularities of morphological contour as to lose touch with their formal ground-plan. Sound changes work mechanically. Hence they are likely to affect a whole morphological group here—this does not matter—, only part of a morphological group there—and this may be disturbing. Thus, the old Anglo-Saxon paradigm:

	Sing.	Plur.
N. Ac.	fot	fet (older foti)
G.	fotes	fota
D.	fet (older foti)	fotum

could not long stand unmodified. The *o—e* alternation was welcome in so far as it roughly distinguished the singular from the plural. The dative singular *fet*, however, though justified historically, was soon felt to be an intrusive feature. The analogy of simpler and more numerously represented paradigms created the form *fote* (compare, e.g., *fisc* "fish," dative singular *fisce*). *Fet* as a dative becomes obsolete. The singular now had *o* throughout. But this very fact made the genitive and dative *o*-forms of the plural seem out of place. The nominative and accusative *fet* was naturally far more frequently in use than were the corresponding forms of the genitive and dative. These, in the end, could not but follow the analogy of *fet*. At the very beginning of the Middle English period, therefore, we find that the old paradigm has yielded to a more regular one:

	Sing.	Plur.
N. Ac.	* fot	* fet
G.	* fotes	fete
D.	fote	feten

The starred forms are the old nucleus around which the new paradigm is built. The unstarred forms are not genealogical kin of their formal prototypes. They are analogical replacements.

The history of the English language teems with such levelings or extensions. *Elder* and *eldest* were at one time the only possible comparative and superlative forms of *old* (compare German *alt, älter, der älteste*; the vowel following the *old-, alt-* was originally an *i*, which modified the quality of the stem vowel). The general analogy of the vast majority of English adjectives, however, has caused the replacement of the forms *elder* and *eldest* by the forms with unmodified vowel, *older* and *oldest*. *Elder* and *eldest* survive only as somewhat archaic terms for the older and oldest brother or sister. This illustrates the tendency for words that are psychologically disconnected from their etymological or formal group to preserve traces of phonetic laws that have otherwise left no recognizable trace or to preserve a vestige of a morphological process that has long lost its vitality. A careful study of these survivals or atrophied forms is not without value for the reconstruction of the earlier history of a language or for suggestive hints as to its remoter affiliations.

Analogy may not only refashion forms within the confines of a related cluster of forms (a "paradigm") but may extend its influence far beyond. Of a number of functionally equivalent elements, for instance, only one may survive, the rest yielding to its constantly widening influence. This is what happened with the English -s plural. Originally confined to a particular class of masculines, though an important class, the -s plural was gradually generalized for all nouns but a mere handful that still illustrate plural types now all but extinct (*foot*: *feet*, *goose*: *geese*, *tooth*: *teeth*, *mouse*: *mice*, *louse*: *lice*; *ox*: *oxen*; *child*: *children*; *sheep*: *sheep*, *deer*: *deer*). Thus analogy not only regularizes irregularities that have come in the wake of phonetic processes but introduces disturbances, generally in favor of greater simplicity or regularity, in a long established system of forms. These analogical adjustments are practically always symptoms of the general morphological drift of the language.

A morphological feature that appears as the incidental consequence of a phonetic process, like the English plural with modified vowel, may spread by analogy no less readily than old features that owe their origin to other than phonetic causes. Once the *e*-vowel of Middle English *fet* had become confined to the plural, there was no theoretical reason why alternations of the type *fot*: *fet* and *mus*: *mis* might not have become established as a productive type of number distinction in the noun. As a matter of fact, it did not so become established. The *fot*: *fet* type of plural secured but a momentary foothold. It was swept into being by one of the surface drifts of the language, to be swept aside in the Middle English period by the more powerful drift toward the use of simple distinctive forms. It was too late in the day for our language to be seriously interested in such pretty symbolisms as *foot*: *feet*. What examples of the type arose legitimately, in other words *via* purely phonetic processes, were tolerated for a time, but the type as such never had a serious future.

It was different in German. The whole series of phonetic changes comprised under the term "umlaut," of which *u: ü* and *au: oi* (written *äu*) are but specific examples, struck the German language at a time when the general drift to morphological simplification was not so strong but that the resulting formal types (e.g., *Fuss: Füsse*; *fallen* "to fall": *fällen* "to fell"; *Horn* "horn": *Gehörne* "group of horns"; *Haus* "house": *Häuslein* "little house") could keep themselves intact and even extend to forms that did not legitimately come within their sphere of influence. "Umlaut" is still a very live symbolic process in German, possibly more alive to-day than in medieval times. Such analogical plurals as *Baum* "tree": *Bäume* (contrast Middle High German *boum: boume*) and derivatives as *lachen* "to laugh": *Gelächter* "laughter" (contrast Middle High German *gelach*) show that vocalic mutation has won through to the status of a productive morphologic process. Some of the dialects have even gone further than standard German, at least in certain respects. In Yiddish, for instance, "umlaut" plurals have been formed where there are no Middle High German prototypes or modern literary parallels, e.g., *tog* "day": *teg* "days" (but German *Tag: Tage*) on the analogy of *gast* "guest": *gest* "guests" (German *Gast: Gäste*), *shuch* "shoe": *shich* "shoes" (but German *Schuh: Schuhe*) on the analogy of *fus* "foot": *fis* "feet." It is possible that "umlaut" will run its course and cease to operate as a live functional process in German, but that time is still distant. Meanwhile all consciousness of the merely phonetic nature of "umlaut" vanished centuries ago. It is now a strictly morphological process, not in the least a mechanical phonetic adjustment. We have in it a splendid example of how a simple phonetic law, meaningless in itself, may eventually color or transform large reaches of the morphology of a language.

How Languages Influence Each Other

Languages, like cultures, are rarely sufficient unto themselves. The necessities of intercourse bring the speakers of one language into direct or indirect contact with those of neighboring or culturally dominant languages. The intercourse may be friendly or hostile. It may move on the humdrum plane of business and trade relations or it may consist of a borrowing or interchange of spiritual goods—art, science, religion. It would be difficult to point to a completely isolated language or dialect, least of all among the primitive peoples. The tribe is often so small that intermarriages with alien tribes that speak other dialects or even totally unrelated languages are not uncommon. It may even be doubted whether intermarriage, intertribal trade, and general cultural interchanges are not of greater relative significance on primitive levels than on our own. Whatever the degree or nature of contact between neighboring peoples, it is generally sufficient to lead to some kind of linguistic interinfluencing. Frequently the influence runs heavily in one direction. The language of a people that is looked upon as a center of culture is naturally far more likely to exert an appreciable influence on other languages spoken in its vicinity than to be influenced by them. Chinese has flooded the vocabularies of Corean, Japanese, and Annamite for centuries, but has received nothing in return. In the western Europe of medieval and modern times French has exercised a similar, though probably a less overwhelming, influence. English borrowed an immense number of words from the French of the Norman invaders, later also from the court French of Isle de France, appropriated a certain number of affixed elements of derivational value (e.g., *-ess* of *princess*, *-ard* of *drunkard*, *-ty* of *royalty*), may have been somewhat stimulated in its general analytic drift by contact with French, and even allowed French to modify its phonetic pattern slightly (e.g., initial *v* and *j* in words like *veal* and *judge*; in words of Anglo-Saxon origin *v* and *j* can only occur after vowels, e.g., *over*, *hedge*). But English has exerted practically no influence on French.

The simplest kind of influence that one language may exert on another is the "borrowing" of words. When there is cultural borrowing there is always the likelihood that the associated words may be borrowed too. When the early Germanic peoples of northern Europe first learned of wine-culture and of paved streets from their commercial or warlike contact with the Romans, it was only natural that they should adopt the Latin words for the strange beverage (*vinum*, English *wine*, German *Wein*) and the unfamiliar type of road (*strata [via]*, English *street*, German *Strasse*). Later, when Christianity was introduced into England, a number of associated words, such as *bishop* and *angel*, found their way into English. And so the process has continued uninterruptedly down to the present day, each cultural wave bringing to the language a new deposit of loan-words. The careful study of such loan-words constitutes an interesting commentary on the history of culture. One can almost estimate the rôle which various peoples have played in the development and spread of cultural ideas by taking note of the extent to which their vocabularies have filtered into those of other peoples. When we realize that an educated Japanese can hardly frame a single literary sentence without the use of Chinese resources, that to this day Siamese and Burmese and Cambodgian bear the unmistakable imprint of the Sanskrit and Pali that came in with Hindu Buddhism centuries ago, or that whether we argue for or against the teaching of Latin and Greek our argument is sure to be studded with words that have come to us from Rome and Athens, we get some inkling of what early Chinese culture and Buddhism and classical Mediterranean civilization have meant in the world's history. There are just five languages that have had an overwhelming significance as carriers of culture. They are classical Chinese, Sanskrit, Arabic, Greek, and Latin. In comparison with these even such culturally important languages as Hebrew and French sink into a secondary position. It is a little disappointing to learn that the general cultural influence of English has so far been all but negligible. The English language itself is spreading because the English have colonized immense territories. But there is nothing to show that it is anywhere entering into the lexical heart of other languages as French has colored the English complexion or as Arabic has permeated Persian and Turkish. This fact alone is significant of the power of nationalism, cultural as well as political, during the last century. There are now psychological resistances to borrowing, or rather to new sources of borrowing, [165] that were not greatly alive in the Middle Ages or during the Renaissance.

Are there resistances of a more intimate nature to the borrowing of words? It is generally assumed that the nature and extent of borrowing depend entirely on the historical facts of culture relation; that if German, for instance, has borrowed less copiously than English from Latin and French it is only because Germany has had less intimate relations than England with the culture spheres of classical Rome and France. This is true to a considerable extent, but it is not the whole truth. We must not exaggerate the physical importance of the Norman invasion nor underrate the significance of the fact that Germany's central geographical position made it peculiarly sensitive to French influences all through the Middle Ages, to humanistic influences in the latter fifteenth and early sixteenth centuries, and again to the powerful French influences of the seventeenth and eighteenth centuries. It seems very probable that the psychological attitude of the borrowing language itself towards linguistic material has much to do with its receptivity to foreign words. English has long been striving for the completely unified, unanalyzed word, regardless of whether it is monosyllabic or polysyllabic. Such words as *credible, certitude, intangible* are entirely welcome in English because each represents a unitary, well-nuanced idea and because their formal analysis (*cred-ible, cert-itude, in-tang-ible*) is not a necessary act of the unconscious mind (*cred-, cert-,* and *tang-* have no real existence in English comparable to that of *good-* in *goodness*). A word like *intangible,* once it is acclimated, is nearly as simple a psychological entity as any radical monosyllable (say *vague, thin, grasp*). In German, however, polysyllabic words strive to analyze themselves into significant elements. Hence vast numbers of French and Latin words, borrowed at the height of certain cultural influences, could not maintain themselves in the language. Latin-German words like *kredibel* "credible" and French-German words like *reussieren* "to succeed" offered nothing that the unconscious mind could assimilate to its customary method of feeling and handling words. It is as though this unconscious mind said: "I am perfectly willing to accept *kredibel* if you will just tell me what you mean by *kred-*." Hence German has generally found it easier to create new words out of its own resources, as the necessity for them arose.

The psychological contrast between English and German as regards the treatment of foreign material is a contrast that may be studied in all parts of the world. The Athabaskan languages of America are spoken by peoples that have had astonishingly varied cultural contacts, yet nowhere do we find that an Athabaskan dialect has borrowed at all freely [[166]] from a neighboring language. These languages have always found it easier to create new words by compounding afresh elements ready to hand. They have for this reason been highly resistant to receiving the linguistic impress of the external cultural experiences of their speakers. Cambodgian and Tibetan offer a highly instructive contrast in their reaction to Sanskrit influence. Both are analytic languages, each totally different from the highly-wrought, inflective language of India. Cambodgian is isolating, but, unlike Chinese, it contains many polysyllabic words whose etymological analysis does not matter. Like English, therefore, in its relation to French and Latin, it welcomed immense numbers of Sanskrit loan-words, many of which are in common use to-day. There was no psychological resistance to them. Classical Tibetan literature was a slavish adaptation of Hindu Buddhist literature and nowhere has Buddhism implanted itself more firmly than in Tibet, yet it is strange how few Sanskrit words have found their way into the language. Tibetan was highly resistant to the polysyllabic words of Sanskrit because they could not automatically fall into significant syllables, as they should have in order to satisfy the Tibetan feeling for form. Tibetan was therefore driven to translating the great majority of these Sanskrit words into native equivalents. The Tibetan craving for form was satisfied, though the literally translated foreign terms must often have done violence to genuine Tibetan idiom. Even the proper names of the Sanskrit originals were carefully translated, element for element, into Tibetan; e.g., *Suryagarbha* "Sun-bosomed" was carefully Tibetanized into *Nyi-mai snying-po* "Sun-of heart-the, the heart (or essence) of the sun." The study of how a language reacts to the presence of foreign words—rejecting them, translating them, or freely accepting them—may throw much valuable light on its innate formal tendencies.

    The borrowing of foreign words always entails their phonetic modification. There are sure to be foreign sounds or accentual peculiarities that do not fit the native phonetic habits. They are then so changed as to do as little violence as possible to these habits. Frequently we have phonetic compromises. Such an English word as the recently introduced *camouflage*, as now ordinarily pronounced, corresponds to the typical phonetic usage of neither English nor French. The aspirated *k*, the obscure vowel of the second syllable, the precise quality of the *l* and of the last *a*, and, above all, the strong accent on the first syllable, are all the results of unconscious assimilation to our English habits of pronunciation. They differentiate our *camouflage* clearly from the same word as pronounced by the French. On the other hand, the long, heavy vowel in the third syllable and the final position of the "zh" sound (like *z* in *azure*) are distinctly un-English, just as, in Middle English, the initial *j* and *v* [167] must have been felt at first as not strictly in accord with English usage, though the strangeness has worn off by now. In all four of these cases—initial *j*, initial *v*, final "zh," and unaccented *a* of *father*—English has not taken on a new sound but has merely extended the use of an old one.

Occasionally a new sound is introduced, but it is likely to melt away before long. In Chaucer's day the old Anglo-Saxon *ü* (written *y*) had long become unrounded to *i*, but a new set of *ü*-vowels had come in from the French (in such words as *due, value, nature*). The new *ü* did not long hold its own; it became diphthongized to *iu* and was amalgamated with the native *iw* of words like *new* and *slew*. Eventually this diphthong appears as *yu*, with change of stress—*dew* (from Anglo-Saxon *deaw*) like *due* (Chaucerian *dü*). Facts like these show how stubbornly a language resists radical tampering with its phonetic pattern.

Nevertheless, we know that languages do influence each other in phonetic respects, and that quite aside from the taking over of foreign sounds with borrowed words. One of the most curious facts that linguistics has to note is the occurrence of striking phonetic parallels in totally unrelated or very remotely related languages of a restricted geographical area. These parallels become especially impressive when they are seen contrastively from a wide phonetic perspective. Here are a few examples. The Germanic languages as a whole have not developed nasalized vowels. Certain Upper German (Suabian) dialects, however, have now nasalized vowels in lieu of the older vowel + nasal consonant (*n*). Is it only accidental that these dialects are spoken in proximity to French, which makes abundant use of nasalized vowels? Again, there are certain general phonetic features that mark off Dutch and Flemish in contrast, say, to North German and Scandinavian dialects. One of these is the presence of unaspirated voiceless stops (*p, t, k*), which have a precise, metallic quality reminiscent of the corresponding French sounds, but which contrast with the stronger, aspirated stops of English, North German, and Danish. Even if we assume that the unaspirated stops are more archaic, that they are the unmodified descendants of the old Germanic consonants, is it not perhaps a significant historical fact that the Dutch dialects, neighbors of French, were inhibited from modifying these consonants in accordance with what seems to have been a general Germanic phonetic drift? Even more striking than these instances is the peculiar resemblance, in certain special phonetic respects, of Russian and other Slavic languages to the unrelated Ural-Altaic languages [168] of the Volga region. The peculiar, dull vowel, for instance, known in Russian as "yeri" [169] has Ural-Altaic analogues, but is entirely wanting in Germanic, Greek, Armenian, and Indo-Iranian, the nearest Indo-European congeners of Slavic. We may at least suspect that the Slavic vowel is not historically unconnected with its Ural-Altaic parallels. One of the most puzzling cases of phonetic parallelism is afforded by a large number of American Indian languages spoken west of the Rockies. Even at the most radical estimate there are at least four totally unrelated linguistic stocks represented in the region from southern Alaska to central California. Nevertheless all, or practically all, the languages of this immense area have some important phonetic features in common. Chief of these is the presence of a "glottalized" series of stopped consonants of very distinctive formation and of quite unusual acoustic effect. [170] In the northern part of the area all the languages, whether related or not, also possess various voiceless *l*-sounds and a series of "velar" (back-guttural) stopped consonants which are etymologically distinct from the ordinary *k*-series. It is difficult to believe that three such peculiar phonetic features as I have mentioned could have evolved independently in neighboring groups of languages.

How are we to explain these and hundreds of similar phonetic convergences? In particular cases we may really be dealing with archaic similarities due to a genetic relationship that it is beyond our present power to demonstrate. But this interpretation will not get us far. It must be ruled entirely out of court, for instance, in two of the three European examples I have instanced; both nasalized vowels and the Slavic "yeri" are demonstrably of secondary origin in Indo-European. However we envisage the process in detail, we cannot avoid the inference that there is a tendency for speech sounds or certain distinctive manners of articulation to spread over a continuous area in somewhat the same way that elements of culture ray out from a geographical center. We may suppose that individual variations arising at linguistic borderlands—whether by the unconscious suggestive influence of foreign speech habits or by the actual transfer of foreign sounds into the speech of bilingual individuals—have gradually been incorporated into the phonetic drift of a language. So long as its main phonetic concern is the preservation of its sound patterning, not of its sounds as such, there is really no reason why a language may not unconsciously assimilate foreign sounds that have succeeded in worming their way into its gamut of individual variations, provided always that these new variations (or reinforced old variations) are in the direction of the native drift.

A simple illustration will throw light on this conception. Let us suppose that two neighboring and unrelated languages, A and B, each possess voiceless *l*-sounds (compare Welsh *ll*). We surmise that this is not an accident. Perhaps comparative study reveals the fact that in language A the voiceless *l*-sounds correspond to a sibilant series in other related languages, that an old alternation *s: sh* has been shifted to the new alternation *l* (voiceless): *s*. Does it follow that the voiceless *l* of language B has had the same history? Not in the least. Perhaps B has a strong tendency toward audible breath release at the end of a word, so that the final *l*, like a final vowel, was originally followed by a marked aspiration. Individuals perhaps tended to anticipate a little the voiceless release and to "unvoice" the latter part of the final *l*-sound (very much as the *l* of English words like *felt* tends to be partly voiceless in anticipation of the voicelessness of the *t*). Yet this final *l* with its latent tendency to unvoicing might never have actually developed into a fully voiceless *l* had not the presence of voiceless *l*-sounds in A acted as an unconscious stimulus or suggestive push toward a more radical change in the line of B's own drift. Once the final voiceless *l* emerged, its alternation in related words with medial voiced *l* is very likely to have led to its analogical spread. The result would be that both A and B have an important phonetic trait in common. Eventually their phonetic systems, judged as mere assemblages of sounds, might even become completely assimilated to each other, though this is an extreme case hardly ever realized in practice. The highly significant thing about such phonetic interinfluencings is the strong tendency of each language to keep its phonetic pattern intact. So long as the respective alignments of the similar sounds is different, so long as they have differing "values" and "weights" in the unrelated languages, these languages cannot be said to have diverged materially from the line of their inherent drift. In phonetics, as in vocabulary, we must be careful not to exaggerate the importance of interlinguistic influences.

I have already pointed out in passing that English has taken over a certain number of morphological elements from French. English also uses a number of affixes that are derived from Latin and Greek. Some of these foreign elements, like the *-ize* of *materialize* or the *-able* of *breakable,* are even productive to-day. Such examples as these are hardly true evidences of a morphological influence exerted by one language on another. Setting aside the fact that they belong to the sphere of derivational concepts and do not touch the central morphological problem of the expression of relational ideas, they have added nothing to the structural peculiarities of our language. English was already prepared for the relation of *pity* to *piteous* by such a native pair as *luck* and *lucky*; *material* and *materialize* merely swelled the ranks of a form pattern familiar from such instances as *wide* and *widen*. In other words, the morphological influence exerted by foreign languages on English, if it is to be gauged by such examples as I have cited, is hardly different in kind from the mere borrowing of words. The introduction of the suffix *-ize* made hardly more difference to the essential build of the language than did the mere fact that it incorporated a given number of words. Had English evolved a new future on the model of the synthetic future in French or had it borrowed from Latin and Greek their employment of reduplication as a functional device (Latin *tango*: *tetigi*; Greek *leipo*: *leloipa*), we should have the right to speak of true morphological influence. But such far-reaching influences are not demonstrable. Within the whole course of the history of the English language we can hardly point to one important morphological change that was not determined by the native drift, though here and there we may surmise that this drift was hastened a little by the suggestive influence of French forms. [172]

It is important to realize the continuous, self-contained morphological development of English and the very modest extent to which its fundamental build has been affected by influences from without. The history of the English language has sometimes been represented as though it relapsed into a kind of chaos on the arrival of the Normans, who proceeded to play nine-pins with the Anglo-Saxon tradition. Students are more conservative today. That a far-reaching analytic development may take place without such external foreign influence as English was subjected to is clear from the history of Danish, which has gone even further than English in certain leveling tendencies. English may be conveniently used as an *a fortiori* test. It was flooded with French loan-words during the later Middle Ages, at a time when its drift toward the analytic type was especially strong. It was therefore changing rapidly both within and on the surface. The wonder, then, is not that it took on a number of external morphological features, mere accretions on its concrete inventory, but that, exposed as it was to remolding influences, it remained so true to its own type and historic drift. The experience gained from the study of the English language is strengthened by all that we know of documented linguistic history. Nowhere do we find any but superficial morphological interinfluencings. We may infer one of several things from this:—That a really serious morphological influence is not, perhaps, impossible, but that its operation is so slow that it has hardly ever had the chance to incorporate itself in the relatively small portion of linguistic history that lies open to inspection; or that there are certain favorable conditions that make for profound morphological disturbances from without, say a peculiar instability of linguistic type or an unusual degree of cultural contact, conditions that do not happen to be realized in our documentary material; or, finally, that we have not the right to assume that a language may easily exert a remolding morphological influence on another.

Meanwhile we are confronted by the baffling fact that important traits of morphology are frequently found distributed among widely differing languages within a large area, so widely differing, indeed, that it is customary to consider them genetically unrelated. Sometimes we may suspect that the resemblance is due to a mere convergence, that a similar morphological feature has grown up independently in unrelated languages. Yet certain morphological distributions are too specific in character to be so lightly dismissed. There must be some historical factor to account for them. Now it should be remembered that the concept of a "linguistic stock" is never definitive [173] in an exclusive sense. We can only say, with reasonable certainty, that such and such languages are descended from a common source, but we cannot say that such and such other languages are not genetically related. All we can do is to say that the evidence for relationship is not cumulative enough to make the inference of common origin absolutely necessary. May it not be, then, that many instances of morphological similarity between divergent languages of a restricted area are merely the last vestiges of a community of type and phonetic substance that the destructive work of diverging drifts has now made unrecognizable?

There is probably still enough lexical and morphological resemblance between modern English and Irish to enable us to make out a fairly conclusive case for their genetic relationship on the basis of the present-day descriptive evidence alone. It is true that the case would seem weak in comparison to the case that we can actually make with the help of the historical and the comparative data that we possess. It would not be a bad case nevertheless. In another two or three millennia, however, the points of resemblance are likely to have become so obliterated that English and Irish, in the absence of all but their own descriptive evidence, will have to be set down as "unrelated" languages. They will still have in common certain fundamental morphological features, but it will be difficult to know how to evaluate them. Only in the light of the contrastive perspective afforded by still more divergent languages, such as Basque and Finnish, will these vestigial resemblances receive their true historic value.

I cannot but suspect that many of the more significant distributions of morphological similarities are to be explained as just such vestiges. The theory of "borrowing" seems totally inadequate to explain those fundamental features of structure, hidden away in the very core of the linguistic complex, that have been pointed out as common, say, to Semitic and Hamitic, to the various Soudanese languages, to Malayo-Polynesian and Mon-Khmer [174] and Munda, [175] to Athabaskan and Tlingit and Haida. We must not allow ourselves to be frightened away by the timidity of the specialists, who are often notably lacking in the sense of what I have called "contrastive perspective."

Attempts have sometimes been made to explain the distribution of these fundamental structural features by the theory of diffusion. We know that myths, religious ideas, types of social organization, industrial devices, and other features of culture may spread from point to point, gradually making themselves at home in cultures to which they were at one time alien. We also know that words may be diffused no less freely than cultural elements, that sounds also may be "borrowed," and that even morphological elements may be taken over. We may go further and recognize that certain languages have, in all probability, taken on structural features owing to the suggestive influence of neighboring languages. An examination of such cases, [176] however, almost invariably reveals the significant fact that they are but superficial additions on the morphological kernel of the language. So long as such direct historical testimony as we have gives us no really convincing examples of profound morphological influence by diffusion, we shall do well not to put too much reliance in diffusion theories. On the whole, therefore, we shall ascribe the major concordances and divergences in linguistic form—phonetic pattern and morphology—to the autonomous drift of language, not to the complicating effect of single, diffused features that cluster now this way, now that. Language is probably the most self-contained, the most massively resistant of all social phenomena. It is easier to kill it off than to disintegrate its individual form.

X

Language, Race and Culture

Language has a setting. The people that speak it belong to a race (or a number of races), that is, to a group which is set off by physical characteristics from other groups. Again, language does not exist apart from culture, that is, from the socially inherited assemblage of practices and beliefs that determines the texture of our lives. Anthropologists have been in the habit of studying man under the three rubrics of race, language, and culture. One of the first things they do with a natural area like Africa or the South Seas is to map it out from this threefold point of view. These maps answer the questions: What and where are the major divisions of the human animal, biologically considered (e.g., Congo Negro, Egyptian White; Australian Black, Polynesian)? What are the most inclusive linguistic groupings, the "linguistic stocks," and what is the distribution of each (e.g., the Hamitic languages of northern Africa, the Bantu languages of the south; the Malayo-Polynesian languages of Indonesia, Melanesia, Micronesia, and Polynesia)? How do the peoples of the given area divide themselves as cultural beings? what are the outstanding "cultural areas" and what are the dominant ideas in each (e.g., the Mohammedan north of Africa; the primitive hunting, non-agricultural culture of the Bushmen in the south; the culture of the Australian natives, poor in physical respects but richly developed in ceremonialism; the more advanced and highly specialized culture of Polynesia)?

The man in the street does not stop to analyze his position in the general scheme of humanity. He feels that he is the representative of some strongly integrated portion of humanity—now thought of as a "nationality," now as a "race"—and that everything that pertains to him as a typical representative of this large group somehow belongs together. If he is an Englishman, he feels himself to be a member of the "Anglo-Saxon" race, the "genius" of which race has fashioned the English language and the "Anglo-Saxon" culture of which the language is the expression. Science is colder. It inquires if these three types of classification—racial, linguistic, and cultural—are congruent, if their association is an inherently necessary one or is merely a matter of external history. The answer to the inquiry is not encouraging to "race" sentimentalists. Historians and anthropologists find that races, languages, and cultures are not distributed in parallel fashion, that their areas of distribution intercross in the most bewildering fashion, and that the history of each is apt to follow a distinctive course. Races intermingle in a way that languages do not. On the other hand, languages may spread far beyond their original home, invading the territory of new races and of new culture spheres. A language may even die out in its primary area and live on among peoples violently hostile to the persons of its original speakers. Further, the accidents of history are constantly rearranging the borders of culture areas without necessarily effacing the existing linguistic cleavages. If we can once thoroughly convince ourselves that race, in its only intelligible, that is biological, sense, is supremely indifferent to the history of languages and cultures, that these are no more directly explainable on the score of race than on that of the laws of physics and chemistry, we shall have gained a viewpoint that allows a certain interest to such mystic slogans as Slavophilism, Anglo-Saxondom, Teutonism, and the Latin genius but that quite refuses to be taken in by any of them. A careful study of linguistic distributions and of the history of such distributions is one of the driest of commentaries on these sentimental creeds.

That a group of languages need not in the least correspond to a racial group or a culture area is easily demonstrated. We may even show how a single language intercrosses with race and culture lines. The English language is not spoken by a unified race. In the United States there are several millions of negroes who know no other language. It is their mother-tongue, the formal vesture of their inmost thoughts and sentiments. It is as much their property, as inalienably "theirs," as the King of England's. Nor do the English-speaking whites of America constitute a definite race except by way of contrast to the negroes. Of the three fundamental white races in Europe generally recognized by physical anthropologists—the Baltic or North European, the Alpine, and the Mediterranean—each has numerous English-speaking representatives in America. But does not the historical core of English-speaking peoples, those relatively "unmixed" populations that still reside in England and its colonies, represent a race, pure and single? I cannot see that the evidence points that way. The English people are an amalgam of many distinct strains. Besides the old "Anglo-Saxon," in other words North German, element which is conventionally represented as the basic strain, the English blood comprises Norman French, [177] Scandinavian, "Celtic," [178] and pre-Celtic elements. If by "English" we mean also Scotch and Irish, [179] then the term "Celtic" is loosely used for at least two quite distinct racial elements—the short, dark-complexioned type of Wales and the taller, lighter, often ruddy-haired type of the Highlands and parts of Ireland. Even if we confine ourselves to the Saxon element, which, needless to say, nowhere appears "pure," we are not at the end of our troubles. We may roughly identify this strain with the racial type now predominant in southern Denmark and adjoining parts of northern Germany. If so, we must content ourselves with the reflection that while the English language is historically most closely affiliated with Frisian, in second degree with the other West Germanic dialects (Low Saxon or "Plattdeutsch," Dutch, High German), only in third degree with Scandinavian, the specific "Saxon" racial type that overran England in the fifth and sixth centuries was largely the same as that now represented by the Danes, who speak a Scandinavian language, while the High German-speaking population of central and southern Germany [180] is markedly distinct.

But what if we ignore these finer distinctions and simply assume that the "Teutonic" or Baltic or North European racial type coincided in its distribution with that of the Germanic languages? Are we not on safe ground then? No, we are now in hotter water than ever. First of all, the mass of the German-speaking population (central and southern Germany, German Switzerland, German Austria) do not belong to the tall, blond-haired, long-headed [181] "Teutonic" race at all, but to the shorter, darker-complexioned, short-headed [182] Alpine race, of which the central population of France, the French Swiss, and many of the western and northern Slavs (e.g., Bohemians and Poles) are equally good representatives. The distribution of these "Alpine" populations corresponds in part to that of the old continental "Celts," whose language has everywhere given way to Italic, Germanic, and Slavic pressure. We shall do well to avoid speaking of a "Celtic race," but if we were driven to give the term a content, it would probably be more appropriate to apply it to, roughly, the western portion of the Alpine peoples than to the two island types that I referred to before. These latter were certainly "Celticized," in speech and, partly, in blood, precisely as, centuries later, most of England

and part of Scotland was "Teutonized" by the Angles and Saxons. Linguistically speaking, the "Celts" of to-day (Irish Gaelic, Manx, Scotch Gaelic, Welsh, Breton) are Celtic and most of the Germans of to-day are Germanic precisely as the American Negro, Americanized Jew, Minnesota Swede, and German-American are "English." But, secondly, the Baltic race was, and is, by no means an exclusively Germanic-speaking people. The northernmost "Celts," such as the Highland Scotch, are in all probability a specialized offshoot of this race. What these people spoke before they were Celticized nobody knows, but there is nothing whatever to indicate that they spoke a Germanic language. Their language may quite well have been as remote from any known Indo-European idiom as are Basque and Turkish to-day. Again, to the east of the Scandinavians are non-Germanic members of the race—the Finns and related peoples, speaking languages that are not definitely known to be related to Indo-European at all.

We cannot stop here. The geographical position of the Germanic languages is such [183] as to make it highly probable that they represent but an outlying transfer of an Indo-European dialect (possibly a Celto-Italic prototype) to a Baltic people speaking a language or a group of languages that was alien to Indo-European. [184] Not only, then, is English not spoken by a unified race at present but its prototype, more likely than not, was originally a foreign language to the race with which English is more particularly associated. We need not seriously entertain the idea that English or the group of languages to which it belongs is in any intelligible sense the expression of race, that there are embedded in it qualities that reflect the temperament or "genius" of a particular breed of human beings.

Many other, and more striking, examples of the lack of correspondence between race and language could be given if space permitted. One instance will do for many. The Malayo-Polynesian languages form a well-defined group that takes in the southern end of the Malay Peninsula and the tremendous island world to the south and east (except Australia and the greater part of New Guinea). In this vast region we find represented no less than three distinct races—the Negro-like Papuans of New Guinea and Melanesia, the Malay race of Indonesia, and the Polynesians of the outer islands. The Polynesians and Malays all speak languages of the Malayo-Polynesian group, while the languages of the Papuans belong partly to this group (Melanesian), partly to the unrelated languages ("Papuan") of New Guinea. [185] In spite of the fact that the greatest race cleavage in this region lies between the Papuans and the Polynesians, the major linguistic division is of Malayan on the one side, Melanesian and Polynesian on the other.

As with race, so with culture. Particularly in more primitive levels, where the secondarily unifying power of the "national" [[186]] ideal does not arise to disturb the flow of what we might call natural distributions, is it easy to show that language and culture are not intrinsically associated. Totally unrelated languages share in one culture, closely related languages —even a single language—belong to distinct culture spheres. There are many excellent examples in aboriginal America. The Athabaskan languages form as clearly unified, as structurally specialized, a group as any that I know of. [[187]] The speakers of these languages belong to four distinct culture areas—the simple hunting culture of western Canada and the interior of Alaska (Loucheux, Chipewyan), the buffalo culture of the Plains (Sarcee), the highly ritualized culture of the southwest (Navaho), and the peculiarly specialized culture of northwestern California (Hupa). The cultural adaptability of the Athabaskan-speaking peoples is in the strangest contrast to the inaccessibility to foreign influences of the languages themselves. [[188]] The Hupa Indians are very typical of the culture area to which they belong. Culturally identical with them are the neighboring Yurok and Karok. There is the liveliest intertribal intercourse between the Hupa, Yurok, and Karok, so much so that all three generally attend an important religious ceremony given by any one of them. It is difficult to say what elements in their combined culture belong in origin to this tribe or that, so much at one are they in communal action, feeling, and thought. But their languages are not merely alien to each other; they belong to three of the major American linguistic groups, each with an immense distribution on the northern continent. Hupa, as we have seen, is Athabaskan and, as such, is also distantly related to Haida (Queen Charlotte Islands) and Tlingit (southern Alaska); Yurok is one of the two isolated Californian languages of the Algonkin stock, the center of gravity of which lies in the region of the Great Lakes; Karok is the northernmost member of the Hokan group, which stretches far to the south beyond the confines of California and has remoter relatives along the Gulf of Mexico.

Returning to English, most of us would readily admit, I believe, that the community of language between Great Britain and the United States is far from arguing a like community of culture. It is customary to say that they possess a common "Anglo-Saxon" cultural heritage, but are not many significant differences in life and feeling obscured by the tendency of the "cultured" to take this common heritage too much for granted? In so far as America is still specifically "English," it is only colonially or vestigially so; its prevailing cultural drift is partly towards autonomous and distinctive developments, partly towards immersion in the larger European culture of which that of England is only a particular facet. We cannot deny that the possession of a common language is still and will long continue to be a smoother of the way to a mutual cultural understanding between England and America, but it is very clear that other factors, some of them rapidly cumulative, are working powerfully to counteract this leveling influence. A common language cannot indefinitely set the seal on a common culture when the geographical, political, and economic determinants of the culture are no longer the same throughout its area.

Language, race, and culture are not necessarily correlated. This does not mean that they never are. There is some tendency, as a matter of fact, for racial and cultural lines of cleavage to correspond to linguistic ones, though in any given case the latter may not be of the same degree of importance as the others. Thus, there is a fairly definite line of cleavage between the Polynesian languages, race, and culture on the one hand and those of the Melanesians on the other, in spite of a considerable amount of overlapping.[189] The racial and cultural division, however, particularly the former, are of major importance, while the linguistic division is of quite minor significance, the Polynesian languages constituting hardly more than a special dialectic subdivision of the combined Melanesian-Polynesian group. Still clearer-cut coincidences of cleavage may be found. The language, race, and culture of the Eskimo are markedly distinct from those of their neighbors;[190] in southern Africa the language, race, and culture of the Bushmen offer an even stronger contrast to those of their Bantu neighbors. Coincidences of this sort are of the greatest significance, of course, but this significance is not one of inherent psychological relation between the three factors of race, language, and culture. The coincidences of cleavage point merely to a readily intelligible historical association. If the Bantu and Bushmen are so sharply differentiated in all respects, the reason is simply that the former are relatively recent arrivals in southern Africa. The two peoples developed in complete isolation from each other; their present propinquity is too recent for the slow process of cultural and racial assimilation to have set in very powerfully. As we go back in time, we shall have to assume that relatively scanty populations occupied large territories for untold generations and that contact with other masses of population was not as insistent and prolonged as it later became. The geographical and historical isolation that brought about race differentiations was naturally favorable also to far-reaching variations in language and culture. The very fact that races and cultures which are brought into historical contact tend to assimilate in the long run, while neighboring languages assimilate each other only casually and in superficial respects [191], indicates that there is no profound causal relation between the development of language and the specific development of race and of culture.

But surely, the wary reader will object, there must be some relation between language and culture, and between language and at least that intangible aspect of race that we call "temperament". Is it not inconceivable that the particular collective qualities of mind that have fashioned a culture are not precisely the same as were responsible for the growth of a particular linguistic morphology? This question takes us into the heart of the most difficult problems of social psychology. It is doubtful if any one has yet attained to sufficient clarity on the nature of the historical process and on the ultimate psychological factors involved in linguistic and cultural drifts to answer it intelligently. I can only very briefly set forth my own views, or rather my general attitude. It would be very difficult to prove that "temperament", the general emotional disposition of a people [192], is basically responsible for the slant and drift of a culture, however much it may manifest itself in an individual's handling of the elements of that culture. But granted that temperament has a certain value for the shaping of culture, difficult though it be to say just how, it does not follow that it has the same value for the shaping of language. It is impossible to show that the form of a language has the slightest connection with national temperament. Its line of variation, its drift, runs inexorably in the channel ordained for it by its historic antecedents; it is as regardless of the feelings and sentiments of its speakers as is the course of a river of the atmospheric humors of the landscape. I am convinced that it is futile to look in linguistic structure for differences corresponding to the temperamental variations which are supposed to be correlated with race. In this connection it is well to remember that the emotional aspect of our psychic life is but meagerly expressed in the build of language [193].

Language and our thought-grooves are inextricably interwoven, are, in a sense, one and the same. As there is nothing to show that there are significant racial differences in the fundamental conformation of thought, it follows that the infinite variability of linguistic form, another name for the infinite variability of the actual process of thought, cannot be an index of such significant racial differences. This is only apparently a paradox. The latent content of all languages is the same—the intuitive *science* of experience. It is the manifest form that is never twice the same, for this form, which we call linguistic morphology, is nothing more nor less than a collective *art* of thought, an art denuded of the irrelevancies of individual sentiment. At last analysis, then, language can no more flow from race as such than can the sonnet form.

Nor can I believe that culture and language are in any true sense causally related. Culture may be defined as *what* a society does and thinks. Language is a particular *how* of thought. It is difficult to see what particular causal relations may be expected to subsist between a selected inventory of experience (culture, a significant selection made by society) and the particular manner in which the society expresses all experience. The drift of culture, another way of saying history, is a complex series of changes in society's selected inventory—additions, losses, changes of emphasis and relation. The drift of language is not properly concerned with changes of content at all, merely with changes in formal expression. It is possible, in thought, to change every sound, word, and concrete concept of a language without changing its inner actuality in the least, just as one can pour into a fixed mold water or plaster or molten gold. If it can be shown that culture has an innate form, a series of contours, quite apart from subject-matter of any description whatsoever, we have a something in culture that may serve as a term of comparison with and possibly a means of relating it to language. But until such purely formal patterns of culture are discovered and laid bare, we shall do well to hold the drifts of language and of culture to be non-comparable and unrelated processes. From this it follows that all attempts to connect particular types of linguistic morphology with certain correlated stages of cultural development are vain. Rightly understood, such correlations are rubbish. The merest *coup d'oeil* verifies our theoretical argument on this point. Both simple and complex types of language of an indefinite number of varieties may be found spoken at any desired level of cultural advance. When it comes to linguistic form, Plato walks with the Macedonian swineherd, Confucius with the head-hunting savage of Assam.

It goes without saying that the mere content of language is intimately related to culture. A society that has no knowledge of theosophy need have no name for it; aborigines that had never seen or heard of a horse were compelled to invent or borrow a word for the animal when they made his acquaintance. In the sense that the vocabulary of a language more or less faithfully reflects the culture whose purposes it serves it is perfectly true that the history of language and the history of culture move along parallel lines. But this superficial and extraneous kind of parallelism is of no real interest to the linguist except in so far as the growth or borrowing of new words incidentally throws light on the formal trends of the language. The linguistic student should never make the mistake of identifying a language with its dictionary.

If both this and the preceding chapter have been largely negative in their contentions, I believe that they have been healthily so. There is perhaps no better way to learn the essential nature of speech than to realize what it is not and what it does not do. Its superficial connections with other historic processes are so close that it needs to be shaken free of them if we are to see it in its own right. Everything that we have so far seen to be true of language points to the fact that it is the most significant and colossal work that the human spirit has evolved—nothing short of a finished form of expression for all communicable experience. This form may be endlessly varied by the individual without thereby losing its distinctive contours; and it is constantly reshaping itself as is all art. Language is the most massive and inclusive art we know, a mountainous and anonymous work of unconscious generations.

Language and Literature

Languages are more to us than systems of thought-transference. They are invisible garments that drape themselves about our spirit and give a predetermined form to all its symbolic expression. When the expression is of unusual significance, we call it literature.[194] Art is so personal an expression that we do not like to feel that it is bound to predetermined form of any sort. The possibilities of individual expression are infinite, language in particular is the most fluid of mediums. Yet some limitation there must be to this freedom, some resistance of the medium. In great art there is the illusion of absolute freedom. The formal restraints imposed by the material —paint, black and white, marble, piano tones, or whatever it may be—are not perceived; it is as though there were a limitless margin of elbow-room between the artist's fullest utilization of form and the most that the material is innately capable of. The artist has intuitively surrendered to the inescapable tyranny of the material, made its brute nature fuse easily with his conception.[195] The material "disappears" precisely because there is nothing in the artist's conception to indicate that any other material exists. For the time being, he, and we with him, move in the artistic medium as a fish moves in the water, oblivious of the existence of an alien atmosphere. No sooner, however, does the artist transgress the law of his medium than we realize with a start that there is a medium to obey.

Language is the medium of literature as marble or bronze or clay are the materials of the sculptor. Since every language has its distinctive peculiarities, the innate formal limitations—and possibilities—of one literature are never quite the same as those of another. The literature fashioned out of the form and substance of a language has the color and the texture of its matrix. The literary artist may never be conscious of just how he is hindered or helped or otherwise guided by the matrix, but when it is a question of translating his work into another language, the nature of the original matrix manifests itself at once. All his effects have been calculated, or intuitively felt, with reference to the formal "genius" of his own language; they cannot be carried over without loss or modification.

Croce [196] is therefore perfectly right in saying that a work of literary art can never be translated. Nevertheless literature does get itself translated, sometimes with astonishing adequacy. This brings up the question whether in the art of literature there are not intertwined two distinct kinds or levels of art—a generalized, non-linguistic art, which can be transferred without loss into an alien linguistic medium, and a specifically linguistic art that is not transferable. [197] I believe the distinction is entirely valid, though we never get the two levels pure in practice. Literature moves in language as a medium, but that medium comprises two layers, the latent content of language—our intuitive record of experience—and the particular conformation of a given language—the specific how of our record of experience. Literature that draws its sustenance mainly—never entirely—from the lower level, say a play of Shakespeare's, is translatable without too great a loss of character. If it moves in the upper rather than in the lower level—a fair example is a lyric of Swinburne's—it is as good as untranslatable. Both types of literary expression may be great or mediocre.

There is really no mystery in the distinction. It can be clarified a little by comparing literature with science. A scientific truth is impersonal, in its essence it is untinctured by the particular linguistic medium in which it finds expression. It can as readily deliver its message in Chinese [198] as in English. Nevertheless it must have some expression, and that expression must needs be a linguistic one. Indeed the apprehension of the scientific truth is itself a linguistic process, for thought is nothing but language denuded of its outward garb. The proper medium of scientific expression is therefore a generalized language that may be defined as a symbolic algebra of which all known languages are translations. One can adequately translate scientific literature because the original scientific expression is itself a translation. Literary expression is personal and concrete, but this does not mean that its significance is altogether bound up with the accidental qualities of the medium. A truly deep symbolism, for instance, does not depend on the verbal associations of a particular language but rests securely on an intuitive basis that underlies all linguistic expression. The artist's "intuition," to use Croce's term, is immediately fashioned out of a generalized human experience—thought and feeling—of which his own individual experience is a highly personalized selection. The thought relations in this deeper level have no specific linguistic vesture; the rhythms are free, not bound, in the first instance, to the traditional rhythms of the artist's language. Certain artists whose spirit moves largely in the non-linguistic (better, in the generalized linguistic) layer even find a certain difficulty in getting themselves expressed in the rigidly set terms of their accepted idiom. One feels that they are unconsciously striving for a generalized art language, a literary algebra, that is related to the sum of all known languages as a perfect mathematical symbolism is related to all the roundabout reports of mathematical relations that normal speech is capable of conveying. Their art expression is frequently strained, it sounds at times like a translation from an unknown original—which, indeed, is precisely what it is. These artists—Whitmans and Brownings—impress us rather by the greatness of their spirit than the felicity of their art. Their relative failure is of the greatest diagnostic value as an index of the pervasive presence in literature of a larger, more intuitive linguistic medium than any particular language.

Nevertheless, human expression being what it is, the greatest—or shall we say the most satisfying—literary artists, the Shakespeares and Heines, are those who have known subconsciously to fit or trim the deeper intuition to the provincial accents of their daily speech. In them there is no effect of strain. Their personal "intuition" appears as a completed synthesis of the absolute art of intuition and the innate, specialized art of the linguistic medium. With Heine, for instance, one is under the illusion that the universe speaks German. The material "disappears."

Every language is itself a collective art of expression. There is concealed in it a particular set of esthetic factors—phonetic, rhythmic, symbolic, morphological—which it does not completely share with any other language. These factors may either merge their potencies with those of that unknown, absolute language to which I have referred—this is the method of Shakespeare and Heine—or they may weave a private, technical art fabric of their own, the innate art of the language intensified or sublimated. The latter type, the more technically "literary" art of Swinburne and of hosts of delicate "minor" poets, is too fragile for endurance. It is built out of spiritualized material, not out of spirit. The successes of the Swinburnes are as valuable for diagnostic purposes as the semi-failures of the Brownings. They show to what extent literary art may lean on the collective art of the language itself. The more extreme technical practitioners may so over-individualize this collective art as to make it almost unendurable. One is not always thankful to have one's flesh and blood frozen to ivory.

An artist must utilize the native esthetic resources of his speech. He may be thankful if the given palette of colors is rich, if the springboard is light. But he deserves no special credit for felicities that are the language's own. We must take for granted this language with all its qualities of flexibility or rigidity and see the artist's work in relation to it. A cathedral on the lowlands is higher than a stick on Mont Blanc. In other words, we must not commit the folly of admiring a French sonnet because the vowels are more sonorous than our own or of condemning Nietzsche's prose because it harbors in its texture combinations of consonants that would affright on English soil. To so judge literature would be tantamount to loving "Tristan und Isolde" because one is fond of the timbre of horns. There are certain things that one language can do supremely well which it would be almost vain for another to attempt. Generally there are compensations. The vocalism of English is an inherently drabber thing than the vowel scale of French, yet English compensates for this drawback by its greater rhythmical alertness. It is even doubtful if the innate sonority of a phonetic system counts for as much, as esthetic determinant, as the relations between the sounds, the total gamut of their similarities and contrasts. As long as the artist has the wherewithal to lay out his sequences and rhythms, it matters little what are the sensuous qualities of the elements of his material.

The phonetic groundwork of a language, however, is only one of the features that give its literature a certain direction. Far more important are its morphological peculiarities. It makes a great deal of difference for the development of style if the language can or cannot create compound words, if its structure is synthetic or analytic, if the words of its sentences have considerable freedom of position or are compelled to fall into a rigidly determined sequence. The major characteristics of style, in so far as style is a technical matter of the building and placing of words, are given by the language itself, quite as inescapably, indeed, as the general acoustic effect of verse is given by the sounds and natural accents of the language. These necessary fundamentals of style are hardly felt by the artist to constrain his individuality of expression. They rather point the way to those stylistic developments that most suit the natural bent of the language. It is not in the least likely that a truly great style can seriously oppose itself to the basic form patterns of the language. It not only incorporates them, it builds on them. The merit of such a style as W.H. Hudson's or George Moore's [199] is that it does with ease and economy what the language is always trying to do. Carlylese, though individual and vigorous, is yet not style; it is a Teutonic mannerism. Nor is the prose of Milton and his contemporaries strictly English; it is semi-Latin done into magnificent English words.

It is strange how long it has taken the European literatures to learn that style is not an absolute, a something that is to be imposed on the language from Greek or Latin models, but merely the language itself, running in its natural grooves, and with enough of an individual accent to allow the artist's personality to be felt as a presence, not as an acrobat. We understand more clearly now that what is effective and beautiful in one language is a vice in another. Latin and Eskimo, with their highly inflected forms, lend themselves to an elaborately periodic structure that would be boring in English. English allows, even demands, a looseness that would be insipid in Chinese. And Chinese, with its unmodified words and rigid sequences, has a compactness of phrase, a terse parallelism, and a silent suggestiveness that would be too tart, too mathematical, for the English genius. While we cannot assimilate the luxurious periods of Latin nor the pointilliste style of the Chinese classics, we can enter sympathetically into the spirit of these alien techniques.

I believe that any English poet of to-day would be thankful for the concision that a Chinese poetaster attains without effort. Here is an example: [200]

> Wu-river [201] stream mouth evening sun sink,
> North look Liao-Tung, [202] not see home.
> Steam whistle several noise, sky-earth boundless,
> Float float one reed out Middle-Kingdom.

These twenty-eight syllables may be clumsily interpreted: "At the mouth of the Yangtsze River, as the sun is about to sink, I look north toward Liao-Tung but do not see my home. The steam-whistle shrills several times on the boundless expanse where meet sky and earth. The steamer, floating gently like a hollow reed, sails out of the Middle Kingdom." [203] But we must not envy Chinese its terseness unduly. Our more sprawling mode of expression is capable of its own beauties, and the more compact luxuriance of Latin style has its loveliness too. There are almost as many natural ideals of literary style as there are languages. Most of these are merely potential, awaiting the hand of artists who will never come. And yet in the recorded texts of primitive tradition and song there are many passages of unique vigor and beauty. The structure of the language often forces an assemblage of concepts that impresses us as a stylistic discovery. Single Algonkin words are like tiny imagist poems. We must be careful not to exaggerate a freshness of content that is at least half due to our freshness of approach, but the possibility is indicated none the less of utterly alien literary styles, each distinctive with its disclosure of the search of the human spirit for beautiful form.

Probably nothing better illustrates the formal dependence of literature on language than the prosodic aspect of poetry. Quantitative verse was entirely natural to the Greeks, not merely because poetry grew up in connection with the chant and the dance,[204] but because alternations of long and short syllables were keenly live facts in the daily economy of the language. The tonal accents, which were only secondarily stress phenomena, helped to give the syllable its quantitative individuality. When the Greek meters were carried over into Latin verse, there was comparatively little strain, for Latin too was characterized by an acute awareness of quantitative distinctions. However, the Latin accent was more markedly stressed than that of Greek. Probably, therefore, the purely quantitative meters modeled after the Greek were felt as a shade more artificial than in the language of their origin. The attempt to cast English verse into Latin and Greek molds has never been successful. The dynamic basis of English is not quantity,[205] but stress, the alternation of accented and unaccented syllables. This fact gives English verse an entirely different slant and has determined the development of its poetic forms, is still responsible for the evolution of new forms. Neither stress nor syllabic weight is a very keen psychologic factor in the dynamics of French. The syllable has great inherent sonority and does not fluctuate significantly as to quantity and stress. Quantitative or accentual metrics would be as artificial in French as stress metrics in classical Greek or quantitative or purely syllabic metrics in English. French prosody was compelled to develop on the basis of unit syllable-groups. Assonance, later rhyme, could not but prove a welcome, an all but necessary, means of articulating or sectioning the somewhat spineless flow of sonorous syllables. English was hospitable to the French suggestion of rhyme, but did not seriously need it in its rhythmic economy. Hence rhyme has always been strictly subordinated to stress as a somewhat decorative feature and has been frequently dispensed with. It is no psychologic accident that rhyme came later into English than in French and is leaving it sooner.[206] Chinese verse has developed along very much the same lines as French verse. The syllable is an even more integral and sonorous unit than in French, while quantity and stress are too uncertain to form the basis of a metric system. Syllable-groups—so and so many syllables per rhythmic unit—and rhyme are therefore two of the controlling factors in Chinese prosody. The third factor, the alternation of syllables with level tone and syllables with inflected (rising or falling) tone, is peculiar to Chinese.

To summarize, Latin and Greek verse depends on the principle of contrasting weights; English verse, on the principle of contrasting stresses; French verse, on the principles of number and echo; Chinese verse, on the principles of number, echo, and contrasting pitches. Each of these rhythmic systems proceeds from the unconscious dynamic habit of the language, falling from the lips of the folk. Study carefully the phonetic system of a language, above all its dynamic features, and you can tell what kind of a verse it has developed—or, if history has played pranks with its phychology, what kind of verse it should have developed and some day will.

Whatever be the sounds, accents, and forms of a language, however these lay hands on the shape of its literature, there is a subtle law of compensations that gives the artist space. If he is squeezed a bit here, he can swing a free arm there. And generally he has rope enough to hang himself with, if he must. It is not strange that this should be so. Language is itself the collective art of expression, a summary of thousands upon thousands of individual intuitions. The individual goes lost in the collective creation, but his personal expression has left some trace in a certain give and flexibility that are inherent in all collective works of the human spirit. The language is ready, or can be quickly made ready, to define the artist's individuality. If no literary artist appears, it is not essentially because the language is too weak an instrument, it is because the culture of the people is not favorable to the growth of such personality as seeks a truly individual verbal expression.

www.ingramcontent.com/pod-product-compliance
Lightning Source LLC
Chambersburg PA
CBHW081112080526
44587CB00021B/3556